THE INVESTOR'S GUIDE TO

NEW ISSUES

THE INVESTOR'S GUIDE TO

NEW ISSUES

Profit from flotations and initial public offerings

David Massey

London · Hong Kong · Johannesburg · Melbourne
Singapore · Washington DC

PITMAN PUBLISHING
128 Long Acre, London WC2E 9AN

A Division of Pearson Professional Limited

First published in Great Britain 1995

© Pearson Professional Limited 1995

British Library Cataloguing in Publication Data
A CIP catalogue record for this book can be obtained
from the British Library.

ISBN 0 273 61117 8

3 5 7 9 10 8 6 4 2

Typeset by Pantek Arts, Maidstone, Kent.
Printed and bound in Great Britain by
Biddles Ltd, Guildford and King's Lynn

*The Publishers' policy is to use paper manufactured
from sustainable forests.*

ABOUT THE AUTHOR

David Massey is the City Editor of the AFX
financial wire service news agency, a joint venture between Pearson and Agence France Pressé.
Before becoming a journalist he was a UK equities fund manager and stockbroking analyst.

ACKNOWLEDGEMENTS

I would like to thank Graham Shore of Shore Capital Stockbrokers for his help with this book, and also all the other friends, brokers and analysts who have helped with advice and comments. Any mistakes are of course my own.

CONTENTS

FOREWORD

Events in 1995 in the new issues markets in both the US and UK served to illustrate both the attractions of investing in new issues (IPOs) and some of the less apparent downside risks.

Investors in what is now effectively a global market for the larger new issues had it brought home to them that political risk was not something to consider only when getting into emerging markets. Instead they received an unwelcome shock when the £4bn sale by the UK Government of its remaining stake in power generators National Power and PowerGen was disrupted in the first days of trading by a review of the related electricity distribution sector by regulator OFFER.

The market took fright at this unexpected intervention and feared greater regulation for the sector was on the cards in response to political pressure after the first takeover bid in the utilities privatized several year before materialized.

Investors accustomed to windfall profits on privatization issues had a rude shock when the partly-paid stock opened at a discount to even the lower price paid by the retail buyer. Allegations of insider trading were made against the UK Treasury, reinforced by a very public shifting of blame by the UK Stock Exchange.

The stock later recovered but investors had been taught a salutary lesson; there is no free ride in the new issues market.

The debacle of the power flotation came in a period when an unprecedented number of disasters hit the new issues market, in some cases losing investors 80 per cent of their money, and a warning on the pitfalls of investing in emerging markets was also served by the collapse of the Mexican market.

In contrast, the last two years have seen some of the most successful new issues of all time, especially in the technology sector which has dominated the headlines.

Anyone lucky enough to have been allocated stock in the Netscape IPO in the US (few were, even amongst the most experienced professionals) needed no further illustration of the potential attractions of Initial Public Offerings (IPOs). The issue soared to a price of $75 on its first day, compared with an issue price of $28.

With markets across the world hitting new all-time highs at the time of writing, led by the technology sector run on Wall Street, more and more companies will perceive the attractions of a stock market listing. This will ensure a healthy flow of new issues in which investors can become involved.

INTRODUCTION

The last few years has seen an explosion in the number of new issues in both the established stock markets of the Western World and the emerging economies of South America, the Pacific Rim and even Eastern Europe.

Privatization, pioneered by the Thatcher Government in the UK, is now a largely spent force in the UK with only the Nuclear Electric and British Rail issues still to come, but the trend continues apace both in Europe and emerging markets, with telecoms stocks often the first in a long line of government sponsored issues.

The new issues market has become an increasingly global marketplace with any issue of size in the United States, Great Britain and Europe now marketed routinely on an international basis using the US style IPO model. Issues in the world's emerging markets have followed the same example as the so-called Tiger economies of the Far East seek investment capital from the well-funded pension and investment funds of the mature Western economies.

New issues can be a very profitable form of investment, but the stream of new investment opportunities has also brought with it a number of salutary lessons for investors. The UK, one of the most highly regulated investment environments in the world, has recently seen some spectacular new issue flops, where investors have lost 80 per cent of their money in just a few months. The sudden debacle in Mexico brought home to many investors the risks of overseas and emerging markets – currency depreciation exacerbated the already dismal performance of the market in domestic terms.

Why is it that companies seek a stock market listing? In the case of privatization there can be a political imperative towards private ownership, or the state can merely be demonstrating the motivations of the wider market, but on a bigger scale. One of the reasons for the (initially) disastrous National Power and PowerGen issue in the UK in 1995 was the need of the Tory Government for some £4bn in privatization proceeds.

Other companies come to the market for a variety of reasons.

Many of the smaller new issues of today obtain a listing to provide an exit for the venture capital fund which has backed the company for the last five years. In these cases, and also in that of demergers, a stock market listing is the preferred alternative to a less administratively complicated 'trade sale' only when a better price can be obtained from the marketplace than from the trade. For this reason flotations are far more prevalent when the overall performance of the stock market has been good.

Linked with the domination of the new issues market by venture capital funds (by one measure a good 50 per cent of new issues in the UK in the last two years have been venture capital backed to some extent) is the increasing number of management buyouts (MBOs). This is partly because venture capitalists would prefer to back an MBO of an existing operation and bring it to the market for an exit within five years than go for the far more risky and drawn-out route of providing 'seedcorn' capital – a trend evident also in North America.

Whatever the reasons for the surge in MBO flotations in recent years, the evidence of UK stockbroking firm James Capel's MBO index is that over the long term MBOs outperform the market, perhaps because of the better financial controls and motivation of the management.

The attraction of MBOs highlights the real reason, and the best reason from the investor's point of view, why companies seek a stock market listing. For an ambitious management with a good track record the ability to issue paper (i.e. more stock) to fund future expansion is of critical importance and can result in their company growing much faster than would otherwise be the case. By investing in a new issue investors can be in on the ground floor.

Which raises the crucial question: why invest in new issues?

The new issues market was drawn to the attention of a whole new class of investors in the 1980s in the UK by the privatization boom. There was a political incentive for the right-wing government to get the issues away at a discount to their true value in order to create a class of loyal investors. These people saw significant profits on their privatization holdings, even though allocations had been scaled down due to a deluge of applications, and routinely sold in the first few weeks of trading.

These investors, most of them new to the concept of direct investment in the stock market, had the impression that a new market had been opened up where they could participate on a level playing field with investment professionals. In fact they had been introduced to an age-old tradition in the stock market – stagging. Stagging is the process of applying for a new issue with no intention of becoming a long-term holder but realizing a small profit as early as possible. In the case of the privatizations of the 1980s the stags did themselves no favours – the stocks have been some of the best performers in the market since.

But the political imperative in favour of give-away privatizations no longer exists, and what appears to be a level playing field is of course nothing of the sort. In the UK, Stock Exchange rules state that issues over a certain size (currently £25m, but under review) must have in them a public offer element. Many sponsors consider private clients to be nothing more than a nuisance and prefer to go via the route of placing stock with institutions rather than offering it to the public at large. Placings of stock now significantly outnumber offers for sale in the UK. More sophisticated private investors have realized that applying in the public offer for very popular new issues is pointless as oversubscription results in massive scaling down of allocations to the point where the holdings are not worthwhile. The UK Stock Exchange has proposed to abolish the requirement to offer new isssues to the general public from January 1996.

But there has been a recent new development which has revived the attractions of new issues to private investors, in the UK at least. The intermediaries offer allows private investors to get involved in the institutional marketing of new issues, provides the opportunity of obtaining an attractive allocation of stock and allows aftermarket dealing on near-equal terms.

Does the development of the book building process, over- and under-allocation of stock (the Green Shoe) and stabilization in the aftermarket, all now routinely employed in international Initial Public Offerings (IPOs), mean that stagging is now pointless? Anecdotal evidence would certainly suggest that it is no longer worthwhile stagging very large offers, especially via the route of the public offer for sale. But investors should also bear in mind the performance of the $2.6bn Netscape IPO in the US, which nearly trebled on its first day.

But it is still the case that with smaller issues there can be value to be had. Around a fifth of new issues valued at over £25m in the last two years have seen a premium of 10 per cent or more on their first day – enough to make the effort and risk worthwhile. The problem remains, of course, of getting enough stock in the first place. If an issue is that good it will in all likelihood be over-subscribed.

However, the traditional obsession of some investors with the first day premium of a new issue conceals its other attractions.

The new issues process is unique in stock market terms in that it comes very close to allowing private investors to play on a level playing field with professionals. The caveat applies, of course, that professionals still have greater access to research and even to the stock itself in many circumstances. But the fact that a new issue prospectus is required to contain such detailed information is of great help to the investor.

The annual report of a company does not come close to a new issue prospectus when it comes to giving relevant information, and once a company has been quoted it can be very difficult to obtain information on which to base an investment decision, especially when it comes to smaller companies.

There have in recent years been a fair number of flops, such as Aerostructures Hamble, to balance the star performers of the new issues market. Portfolio theory applies as much, if not more so, to new issues as it does to conventional stocks. No fund manager would have all his eggs in one basket, and neither should the new issues investor.

But despite the well-publicized disasters in recent memory, all the evidence is that a portfolio of new issues will in general outperform the market as a whole. If some basic investment rules are applied to screen out the obviously unattractive or too risky, the ratio of winners to losers can be shifted even more in favour of the investors.

I hope this book will show how to find the winners in the new issues market, avoid some of the losers and maximize profits both in terms of applications and eventually realizing investment gains.

'Equity finance. . . can be much more attractive than debt finance.'

1

WHAT DRIVES THE NEW ISSUE MARKET?

- Attraction of equity finance
- MBOs and venture capital
- Trade sales
- Demergers
- Who are the buyers?

ROLE OF THE STOCK MARKET IN RAISING MONEY

In 1994 companies listed on the UK Stock Exchange raised some £13bn from their investors. In the US. The New York Stock Exchange (NYSE) alone, one of several markets, raised $21.8bn from just domestic issues. Around half of this was from new issues, while the balance was raised by already quoted companies issuing new shares to existing investors.

The vast majority of companies which seek a listing on the Stock Exchange are doing so in order to gain access to this form of finance at some time in the future. Indeed, any company which is not seeking additional equity finance is either highly cash generative or is not looking to expand organically or by acquisition. The latter is generally a signal to avoid the stock as a potential new issue investment unless other considerations such as yield are taken into account.

WHY DO COMPANIES COME TO THE
NEW ISSUE MARKET?

For growing companies, equity finance through a share issue can be much more attractive than debt finance from banks. Rapidly growing smaller companies often suffer pressure on working capital from their need to finance growing order books etc. If they are having to pay interest on debt finance, this would eat up money which could otherwise be reinvested and so restrict the growth of the company.

Equity finance is a more attractive alternative as dividend yields are generally lower than interest rates, especially the higher rates which banks require from smaller companies. Furthermore, it is considered perfectly normal for companies either to pay a very low dividend or not to pay a dividend at all in their first few years of operation. Investors expect their returns later, of course.

But most companies operate on a mixture of equity and debt. To a large extent this is dictated by the lending policies of banks, which on the whole only lend against security and like to see some assets in the company before lending money. The idea, of course, is that the owners of the company lose money before the bank does. So, in order to borrow money in the first place, most companies need some equity in the business.

That said, the attraction of equity finance is almost never the real reason for companies coming to the stock market, although it is of course a genuine benefit. A smaller company can obtain a mixture of equity and debt finance from any number of sources without the need for a market listing, although in practice it usually comes from the venture capital arms of the clearing or merchant banks, or venture capital firms such as 3i (Investors in Industry, itself recently floated on the London Stock Exchange), or APAX Partners in the US, also said to be interested in setting up a European version of the US NASDAQ market to provide a market for venture capital exits, *inter alia*.

Venture capital and MBO exits dominate

The real reason for many new issues is to realize a value and provide an exit for these venture capital firms. Except in a few circumstances, a new company cannot apply for a market listing until it has a trading record of around three years. For much of that time it will probably have been funded by its bankers. It also has to satisfy other criteria.

Relatively few venture capital firms will invest in 'seedcorn' ventures; they will require a trading history before they will finance expansion. When they have invested in a company, an exit is generally sought within five years. The two most common exits which will enable the funds to realize their investment are a trade sale (i.e. to a larger firm in the same industry as the financed venture) or flotation on the stock market.

> **The real reason for many new issues is to realize a value and provide an exit for these venture capital firms.**

Whether the venture capital firm sells all its holding at flotation depends largely on the investment objectives of the fund, but there are also some restrictions. Limited partnerships must in general distribute their holdings to their partners, but other funds do not have to sell, and frequently retain holdings. Insurance company venture capital funds can pass on their investments to the quoted company fund management team, but bank venture capital operations tend to be straight sellers to generate more cash for reinvestment.

In the UK market venture capitalists have jealously protected their right to realize holdings at their discretion. In the US no new issue would get away unless the venture capitalists had agreed to be locked in for some time.

In the two years 1993 and 1994 at least 75 companies came to the market as a result of a sale by a venture capital firm, or were management buyouts (MBOs) coming or returning to the market, more often than not with some form of venture capital backing. The majority of the issues on offer came from these companies especially in the £25m to £300m range into which most new issues fall.

The trend is even more evident in the US, with venture capital firms involved in a large proportion of even the largest IPOs.

Many of these flotations are MBOs returning to the market after only a few years in private hands. This reflects the view of the venture capital funds themselves that it is generally less risky to fund a management buyout which can be brought back to the market after a swift turnaround than to invest in a company at an earlier stage of its development, so-called 'seedcorn' capital. The merits or otherwise of this policy are beyond the scope of the book but it does have a great deal of bearing on the attraction or otherwise of the new issue.

Several large venture capital funds often exert a considerable amount of control over the management of a company and can have their own motivations for bringing a stock to the market. A number of new issues in 1994 came out with profits warnings only a few months after flotation, leading investors to suspect that they may have been rushed to market by major shareholders who had lost confidence in their investment. Other allegations were made that the managers had squeezed the companies very hard in the run up to flotation to maximize their exit price, with later dire consequences for the stocks concerned.

MBOs outperform

Despite the bad publicity generated by a handful of disastrous performances by MBO flotations, the evidence is that MBO flotations generally outperform the market.

Some of the reasons cited for this have been the fact that when taking on an MBO, managers have to conduct due diligence very carefully as it is their money they are risking. The

Over a long period MBOs consistently outperform the market.

companies also have very tight management of working capital and cash flow, vital to service the MBO debt taken on, and are as a result leaner and fitter than some of their counterparts. As the management team usually retains a substantial stake in the company even after flotation, they are consequently well motivated thereafter as well.

UK stockbroking firm James Capel maintains an index of the performance of MBO exits after flotation, which demonstrates that despite the recent dire performance of some stocks, notably McDonnell Information Systems and Aerostructures Hamble, over a long period MBOs consistently outperform the market.

Trade sales

The alternative to a flotation is a trade sale. What motivates vendors to go for a trade sale rather than a flotation? Price certainly plays a part, and the number of trade sales increases dramatically when the performance of the stock market has been poor, and the investment community is not prepared to pay top prices for new issues and vice versa.

When the market is going up every day or institutional cash flow is good, the fund managers are constantly looking for new investments and are less choosy on price. The figures cannot be directly compared as virtually any company can be sold privately provided a buyer can be found whereas only certain companies are suitable for a market listing. However, the evidence tends to indicate that trade sales usually outnumber flotations.

So why go for a listing? A trade sale surrenders the independence of the management, which usually has a significant personal stake in the company, especially in the case of MBOs. Once people have had the chance to run the show they are generally unwilling to surrender their freedom of action, and for ambitious management a share price quote offers a number of possibilities, including that of significant personal wealth if the price performs.

Ambition

The great advantage of a share price quote is that if investors are keen on the company more finance can be raised by further share issues, by way of open offer, placing or rights issue. This finances the expansion of the company, but so does straight bank finance, albeit often at greater cost in the short term. A share price quote also offers the possibility of buying other com-

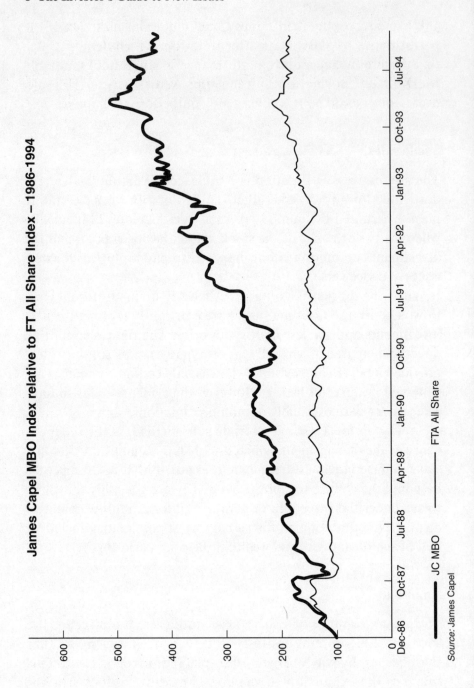

James Capel MBO Index relative to FT All Share Index – 1986-1994

JC MBO ——— FTA All Share

Source: James Capel

panies with paper, i.e. issuing the company's stock to pay for acquisitions. Provided the company has a good story to tell the market, some spectacular growth can be achieved – witness the growth of the F H Tomkins Buckle Company, now FT-SE 100 stock Tomkins, run by ex-Hanson man Greg Hutchings. This is one of the primary attractions of a stock market listing for some managers, and provided they can deliver, the ride can be a profitable one for investors.

Other vendors and demergers

Other stocks come to the market through being demerged from larger parents. This was the case with one of the larger issues of the last two years, the flotation of House of Fraser by the Al-Fayeds, and the largest introduction, the demerger of CAMAS. US parent Tenneco also demerged Albright & Wilson in a $700m global issue.

There has in the 1990s been a trend away from diversification and back towards core markets, which has prompted larger companies to dispose of a large number of non-core assets. But in these cases the question has to be asked why the disposal is taking place. The management of the parent company has almost certainly made an objective decision regarding trade sale or flotation and concluded that a flotation will maximize proceeds, so the price should come under some scrutiny. It might also be alleged that no parent will sell a fast growing or highly cash generative company unless it has a good reason for doing so.

The question which has to be asked of any company floated off by a larger parent is: how much debt is it assuming? The Al-Fayeds sold off House of Fraser because it was necessary in order to reduce debt. They therefore had an incentive to leave the company with as much debt as the issue would stand.

Finance

Finally, there are companies which come to the market solely to finance their own organic (i.e. not acquisition led) expansion, because bank debt alone is either unsuitable or unobtainable in sufficient quantity. These can be major capital projects such as Eurotunnel or cable television companies, which require a vast amount of finance before they are completed, or smaller companies with a growth story to tell, but of which traditional backers are wary. Most of these are high technology or scientific research based stocks, of which there has been a proliferation in recent years after Stock Exchange listing rules were changed to allow them access to the market, following the example of US authorities.

WHO ARE THE BUYERS?

We have seen why companies come to the stock market. What is the motivation for investing in these new issues? For institutional investors, who control well over 70 per cent of the funds in the market, there is cash flow to invest and a regular stream of new issues complements rights issues and other cash raisings as a home for these funds, as well as replacing stocks of those companies which leave the quoted arena through takeovers for cash.

Private investors do not have the same imperatives, as their choice of investments is made more selectively. But for all investors the attraction of new issues is the same: they offer the opportunity to get in on the ground floor with a company, on what is hopefully a level playing field, with access to more information on the company than is otherwise the case in stock market investment.

'A new issue can be brought to the market in four ways. The routes are not mutually exclusive.'

2

TYPES OF NEW ISSUE

- Criteria for listing
- Offers for sale
- What's wrong with privatizations
- Intermediaries offers
- Placings
- Introductions
- New developments
- Timetables
- The US IPO (initial public offering)

HOW DOES A COMPANY ACHIEVE A LISTING?

For a company to achieve a full Stock Exchange listing it must satisfy criteria regarding history, management and shareholders. Special rules apply in the UK for overseas, property companies, those undertaking major capital projects such as Eurotunnel, mineral and scientific research based companies. Different rules apply to the new lightly regulated AIM (Alternative Investment Market) and Rule 4.2 quoted companies.

The basic criteria for a listing are that the company is able to show properly audited accounts with no auditor's qualification for the last three years, and that the latest accounts cover a period ending within the last six months. The company should have been an independent entity with a revenue earning business for at least this three-year period and must have had continuity of management. This requires the current executive directors to have had direct management responsibility of the major businesses for the last three years, and the management team not to have changed materially.

How much has to be raised?

Under current rules as specified by the UK Stock Exchange the required market capitalization of the shares to be listed is only some £700,000, a surprisingly low figure considering that a large proportion of this can be tied up by controlling shareholders or management.

In practice the market capitalization of companies looking for a full listing is almost always significantly higher than £700,000, usually into several millions, not least because of the costs of obtaining and retaining a listing. It is difficult to bring a company to the market for less than £300,000, a sum which makes small listings impractical. Most smaller companies used to opt for the USM (Unlisted Securities Market, soon to expire) and are now more likely to be found on the AIM and Rule 4.2 markets – where the cost could be as little as £50,000.

Generally, at least 25 per cent of the shares must be in public hands, referred to as the free float. Public hands, excludes directors or those

> **At least 25 per cent of the shares must be in public hands,**

connected with directors, the trustees of the employee share option scheme or pension fund and any person with the right to nominate directors. Any person (including company or fund) holding more than 5 per cent of the equity is also excluded from this definition.

If a company sees less than 25 per cent of its shares in public hands it risks the Stock Exchange suspending or cancelling its listing.

Many smaller companies come to the market with a controlling shareholder, that is a holder of more than 30 per cent of the voting rights or the majority of votes at board meetings. The company is supposed to demonstrate to the Stock Exchange that all transactions are at arm's length and that it is independent of its controlling shareholder. Although this is sometimes the case, most investors would remain sceptical. The terms for the buyout of the minority of Rothmans International by Richemont appeared to be quite favourable to the minority, for which investors could thank the independent directors, but Conrad Black's attempts to take *The Daily Telegraph* private ran into a great deal of criticism.

Finally, the company needs two market makers willing to make a market after the issue. At least one of these market makers must be independent, that is not connected to the sponsor handling the issue. An issue with a market capitalization at the offer price of more than £25m must have at least two independent market makers. To ensure that the market makers have sufficient stock to enable a liquid market to operate, at least 5 per cent of any shares placed firm must be offered to them.

A new issue can be brought to the market in one of four ways: by introduction, offer for sale/subscription, placing and intermediaries offer. The routes are not mutually exclusive and several methods are usually combined.

OFFER FOR SALE

The offer for sale is the most publicized method of bringing a company to the market, not least because it involves newspaper advertising and, for the larger issues, press and television advertising campaigns. When mass market advertising is used, investors should consider whether a company which needs to advertise so heavily to attract investment is that attractive. The marketing of a share issue to large numbers of investors who are not otherwise stock market participants may have a political imperative for privatization issues, but in other large issues it would be wise to compare the apparent size of the advertising campaign with the amount of money the company is seeking to raise.

Stock Exchange rules at the time of writing require that any issue over £25m must be marketed partially via an offer for sale, which allows applications by the general public. In the minds of many City advisers this is simply a costly nuisance and they would prefer to market issues solely by a placing. Consequently, in most cases, they use the rules allowing the placing of stock to the full. A consultative document from the Stock Exchange has proposed abolishing the requirement to offer to the general public from January 1996.

An offer for sale differs from an offer for subscription only in that an offer for sale involves shares which have already been issued,

whereas an offer for subscription is for shares not yet in issue. From
the point of view of the purchaser the difference is of largely acade-
mic interest. In either case the offer can be at a fixed price or in the
form of an invitation to tender at or above a stated minimum.

The 'buy side' i.e. fund managers and investors, like fixed price
issues as they know what they are getting and can easily value the
issue when compared with others in the market. Tenders are not a
problem for professional investors,
because they are in touch with
market sentiment as to what the
eventual strike price (the level
chosen by the vendors to maximize
allocations and the sum raised) will

**The offer for sale . . .
permits applications
from the general public.**

be. Private investors are not so impressed with the process, especially when they are expected to tender a sum of money with just a
maximum price limit, as with the BSkyB issue.

In the offer process the share issue must be advertised in at least
two national newspapers. In practice it is now the case that press
and television advertising campaigns accompany the 'off the page'
application forms, together with registration telephone numbers
(all used to build up a database for mailings of further issues).
There is no actual requirement that stock should be offered in the
small parcels of as little as 100 shares which have been common
with privatizations, but smaller and unsophisticated investors have
been deterred by having to invest larger sums of money in the past.

How attractive is an offer for sale

The great advantage of the offer for sale for the private investor is
that it apparently allows a level playing field and permits applications from the general public. All that is required is an application
either by post or handed in in person on a duly completed application form, accompanied by a cheque for the required amount.
Applications for small parcels of stock are generally accepted and
in larger issues there are often special aftermarket discount dealing
schemes set up by banks and broking firms which allow batching
of family orders.

However, the standard offer for sale has a number of serious disadvantages for both the private and institutional investor.

The problem for the institutions is that in certain issues, mainly privatizations, they are artificially denied the allocations of stock they would otherwise want so they can be given to private applicants. Nobody supposes for one minute that a large proportion of these investors will hang on to the stock, but rather they will sell at the first opportunity to realize a small profit – a classic stagging operation.

Institutions, the genuine long-term holders of most of the stock in the market, feel aggrieved that they are forced to buy the stock in the aftermarket from smaller investors, creating artificial first day profits for small stags and the impression of a healthy aftermarket. However, this phenomenon has declined as the desirability of bonanzas for smaller shareholders has eroded and the institutions have been more circumspect in their buying. The political will is now to get the issue away at the price closest to what the market will stand, hence the US-style book building process.

Scaling down

The large-scale offer for sale also has more disadvantages for the private investor than might be evident at first sight. The primary disadvantage is that in heavily publicized and attractive offers applications can be scaled down so heavily that the amount of stock allocated is worthless as a long-term holding – dividend payments of a few pounds a year are merely an irritation – and any profit on the holding is eaten up by dealing costs.

It is not unusual for applications to be scaled down to a holding of less than £500 in value. On a holding of this size even a 10 per cent first day premium (assuming the stock is pointless as a long-term holding and the investor merely wants out) will be severely eroded. Most stocks will have a market maker's spread of 1 per cent and most brokers charge a minimum transaction cost at £25 to £30 – halving the profits on the deal.

Low cost dealing services do of course exist. For ease of dealing and administration, many of these operate a batching system whereby the broker concerned waits until he has a number of orders which make up an amount of stock approaching normal market size. This makes life easier for the broker and consequently cheaper for the client, but can be at the expense of achieving the best price in the market. That said, halving the commission on a small deal is a lot more important in profit terms than an extra penny on the price.

Ballots

Realizing that allocating very small parcels of stock merely results in a wave of small dealings in the first few days of trading, sponsors do on occasion have a ballot to determine allocations. This means that some applicants at random receive a larger proportion of what they have asked for at the expense of others who receive nothing at all. However, it is still the case that in a ballot the amount of stock actually received by the lucky applicants is disappointingly small.

Stagging risks

Investors who decide to stag a new issue which involves a large offer for sale by selling in the first few hours of trading take some considerable risks. Average private client investors cannot be sure how much stock they have been allocated. Even if a ballot has not taken place and they can find out from the market the level of allocations, they take the risk that they have been missed out in the allocation process.

Administrative errors do take place and applications are not always processed – in the Abbey National issue a volume of correspondence was later found to have been thrown away by accident. In these cases the applicants have no right of appeal, as they have offered to buy the stock in the issue. Their offers have not been accepted by the sponsor and therefore no contract has been cemented. Unsuccessful applicants are entitled only to get their cheques back.

Therefore, if investors in an offer for sale sell in the market before knowing the number of shares they have been allocated, they are in fact running the risk of 'going short', i.e. selling stock they do not own. If no stock was ultimately forthcoming they would then have to buy the stock back in the market, almost certainly at a net loss after two sets of dealing costs have been taken into account.

In practice this situation almost never arises as brokers will virtually never sell stock for members of the public without seeing their allotment letters. There are sound commercial reasons for this as it reduces the number of administrative problems, but SFA (Securities and Futures Authority, UK regulators) concerns also prevent them from doing so. Allowing a private investor to potentially go short of an issue would not be considered 'appropriate' for most investors under SFA rules.

The only investors who would be allowed to sell stock without producing an allotment letter would be the more sophisticated and well-known clients of the firm, who in most cases could not be bothered with the small amount of stock in the first place.

Small investors can't deal

This reveals one of the major problems for private investors in an offer for sale – that they cannot in practice deal from the first moment when dealings commence because they must wait for the post to confirm their allocation. The playing field in these issues is far from level because despatch of allotment letters can take anything from a day to two weeks. The situation is exacerbated by the practice of allowing 'Grey Market' dealings in some issues.

Opportunity costs

The other side of the problem of small allocations and heavy scaling down is the loss of interest income on the money used for the application. Offers for sale require a cheque for the full amount to be attached to the application. (It is wise to note exactly the instructions for making the application. In earlier privatizations the word 'pinned' was not considered to have the same meaning as 'stapled', and some applications ran the risk of being rejected.)

Large offers for sale always result in vast outflows of money from building societies – consider that in some cases several hundred million pounds worth of stock is on offer to the general public, who oversubscribe the issue perhaps five times or more.

Return cheques for the balance between stock allocated and that applied for generally accompany the allotment letter – i.e. arriving several days after trading starts and up to three weeks since the last date for applications to be in. Investors lose the interest income on all their money for the period between applications and allocation of stock. In heavily over-subscribed issues investors could potentially apply for £5,000 worth of stock, receive only £1,000 and make a loss after dealing charges on the sale, as well as a further loss of up to a month's interest on their original £5,000.

> **Investors lose the interest income . . . for the period between applications and allocation of stock.**

The administrative burden which a large public offer for sale puts on the issuing house, resulting in an extended offer period, can have other pitfalls. It is traditional in offers for sale for the price to be announced before applications are solicited, although recent developments have changed this.

Apply at the last minute – but only in the UK

The period during which applications are solicited can perhaps last for two weeks, a long time in the stock market, especially if conditions are volatile. The price at which an issue appeared attractive on its impact day can look decidedly over the odds if the market has fallen 500 points by the time first dealings commence. This is unusual but by no means unheard of. It actually happened in the sale of the UK Government's remaining stake in BP in 1987, when the market crashed after the issue was priced but before applications closed. Some investors still queued up to hand in their applications. When dealings commenced the partly paid shares were at a 30 pence discount to their partly paid price, a substantial loss when dealing costs were taken into account. The lesson to be learnt in virtually all fixed price offers for sale is to apply at the last minute as the institutions do. Applications can almost never be pulled (i.e. withdrawn) once made.

This tendency for applications to arrive in a flood at the last minute does nothing for the digestion of corporate financiers who do not know what the level of applications will be until the last minute, at which point it is too late for them to do anything about it. This has been another prompt for the introduction of an amended offer process as imported into the UK from the US.

New developments

The third tranche of the UK Government's sale of its holding in British Telecom (BT3) introduced a number of new developments into the new issue market, mainly to forestall political criticism of the apparent giveaway pricing of some earlier privatizations. However, the disenchantment of larger private clients with the offer for sale process was also taken into account.

Most of the new developments in the UK were imported from the US new issue market which operates on a different basis from that of the UK (see below). The primary import was the book building process, designed to match more closely the expectations of the sponsors to the issue and the institutions who ultimately determine the long-term price performance of the stocks concerned.

Book building

Book building is a more formal version of the institutional marketing process already well known in the UK. Institutions are canvassed for their indications of price and size interest in the new issue well before the price is determined. However, in order to encourage serious indications and discourage the usual last minute flood of applications, the fund managers are told that early expressions of interest will be treated more favourably in allocations than applicants who pile in at the last minute when a premium looks likely. Whether it would ultimately be possible for a sponsor to deny, the UK's largest fund managers their share of stock is open to doubt.

During the book building exercise for the Wellcome issue, institutions were widely thought mistakenly to have driven the price down by 'shorting' the issue, to the discomfort of the sponsors, Robert Fleming. This was rectified in BT3 with the threat that those institutions thought to have shorted the issue during the offer process would not be allocated stock in the issue, and further refined in the National Power and PowerGen issues with the daily publication of the level of open traded option and other interest in the market.

In a US-style book building process the price is only decided at the last minute as allocations are announced. The process is similar to a tender offer for BT3 where institutional investors indicated the price at which they were prepared to buy stock, in stepped levels of interest if desired – i.e. 100,000 shares at 120 pence, 50,000 at 130 pence etc. Once the strike price had been set, they were informed of their entitlements and trading commenced almost immediately.

Prices not fixed

The consequence of this process for private investors was that they did not actually get to know what price they would have to pay for their shares. Application forms in the public offer prospectus indicated the value of stock they wanted to buy and the maximum price they were prepared to pay. Should the issue have been priced at a higher level, no stock would have been allocated. While this does indicate an element of contempt for private investors, they did at least have the incentive that they were buying the stock at a guaranteed discount to the price paid by the institutions.

This process was repeated in the BSkyB flotation where the general public were once again invited to specify the value of the shares they would apply for, with a maximum price stated. However, in this case no discounts for small investors were forthcoming. The success of the BT3 offer would seem to indicate that this is likely to become the model for future large-scale offers for sale.

The advantage of the book building exercise for the institutions is that those who are genuine buyers of the stock can acquire their holdings more efficiently than by buying in the aftermarket, paying dealing costs and possibly forcing the price up. Stags are by no means unknown amongst investment professionals, and many unit trust managers apply for stock in new issues with no intention of becoming long-term holders. The advantage of the process for the sponsor to the issue is the ability to massage the price, to obtain better feedback regarding the level of interest and to move stock between world markets to better reflect investor demand.

Whatever the disadvantages of the process for smaller investors, it was certainly thought to be the case that the BT3 issue came to the market at a price much closer to that which the market could stand than previous offers for sale. That said, in both the BT3 and Wellcome offers, the advisers had an easy price comparison in that the stock was already traded in the market.

However, the most significant development in the BT3 offer was the introduction of the intermediaries offer, which gave the disillusioned larger-scale private investor both the opportunity and the incentive to become involved in these large-scale offers for sale.

The Green Shoe

A common feature of North American new issues is the ability of the issuer to over- or under-allot shares according to demand. This, for obscure reasons, is known as a 'Green Shoe'.

In this process, which must be signalled in the prospectus, the issuer may allot more stock than originally intended or alternatively scale down the issue according to demand to prevent volatile aftermarket prices and achieve the largest practicable fund raising for the company concerned. Over-allotment provisions are of course of great interest to the potential investor as the level of aftermarket demand from unfulfilled institutional applicants is a major determinant of subsequent price performance.

Stabilization

Stabilization is another feature imported into the UK from the US, and allows the sponsor to the issue to manipulate the aftermarket for a limited period. In order to prevent a huge first day premium caused by a stock shortage, the sponsor can over-allot stock with a view to buying it back over the course of the next few weeks when prices have stabilized.

Alternatively, it is possible for the sponsor to buy in stock should the issue fall below its issue price, effectively supporting the price. It should be noted, however, that there is no obligation to support the issue at its issue price, and as the process is generally operated through the market making arm of the house concerned, it is conceivable that a stabilization operation

> It is . . . . not unusual for allocations to be changed at the last minute

to support a price could result in market makers making substantial profits on their books. This was denied by S G Warburg in the case of the BT3 issue. The house concerned has to inform the market that stabilization transactions could be occurring but there is no necessity for formal confirmation.

Global book building

The offer process for a large new issue is now usually managed on a global basis, involving a potentially very large number of broking firms and a global road show to publicize it. It is up to the lead broker in the issue to decide how the book building is done and by whom, but the whole idea of global book building is to ascertain the level of demand from different investment communities.

It is therefore not unusual for allocations to be changed at the last minute if demand is stronger in some markets than others. In the case of UK issues, especially privatizations, it has been commonplace for overseas investors to be denied stock allocations in favour of allotting the shares to UK private investors when demand is high.

INTERMEDIARIES OFFER

The intermediaries offer is also a relatively recent development, evolving out of the dissatisfaction of more sophisticated private

New Issues in the UK with a Public Offer or Intermediaries Offer Element 1994

Company	Method	Raised (£m)
3i Group[1]	IO & PL @ 272p	711.5
Aerostructures Hamble[2]	IO & PL @ 120p	40.0
Alpha Airports[4]	IO & PL @ 140p	158.3
Argent	IO & PL @ 255p	35.0
Ashbourne	IO & PL @ 150p	50.0
Beazer Homes[4]	IO & PL @ 165p	463.4
BSkyB	O/Sub @ 256p	878.1
Capital Shopping Centres	IO & PL @ 230p	298.7
Chamberlain Phipps	IO & PL @ 165p	37.7
Chiroscience	PL & O/S @ 150p	45.0
CLS Holdings	IO & PL @ 111p	50.0
Continental Foods	IO & PL @ 2p	2.1
Copyright Promotions	IO & PL @ 120p	3.6
Denby Group	IO & PL @ 130p	26.5
Eurodollar	IO & PL @ 220p	50.0
Exco	IO & PL @ 175p	92.9
Eyecare Products	IO & PL @ 30p	18.4
Fiscal Properties	IO & PL @ 78p	25.3
Goldsborough Healthcare	IO & PL @ 170p	62.3
Graham Group	O/S & PL @ 183p	209.8
Hamleys	IO & PL @ 185p	19.1
Heathcall Group	IO & PL @ 105p	31.1
Hobson	IO & PL @ 27p	80.0
House of Fraser[4]	IO & PL @ 180p	413.2
Inspec	IO & PL @ 160p	49.5
Intermediate Capital	IO & PL @ 225p	45.0
Irish Permanent	IO & PL @ Ir 180p	54.6
Keller Group	IO & PL @ 130p	44.5
Lombard Insurance[3]	IO & PL @ 160p	33.0
Man (ED & F) Group	IO & PL @ 180p	110.0
McDonnell Information Systems[2]	IO & PL @ 260p	190.1
Midland Assets	IO & PL @ 14p	2.4
Millwall Holdings	IO & PL @ 140p	109.2
Morgan Sindall	IO & PL @ 60p	2.6
Nottingham Group[2]	IO & PL @ 155p	38.0
Orbis	IO & PL @ 23p	4.9

New Issues in the UK with a Public Offer or Intermediaries Offer Element 1994 *continued*

Company	Method	Raised (£m)
Partco	IO & PL @ 200p	29.1
Pillar Property	IO & PL @ 150p	90.0
Pittencrieff	IO & PL @ 100p	27.0
Redrow	IO & PL @ 135p	117.5
Regent Corporation	IO & PL @ 27p	3.3
RJB Mining	O/S & PL @ 320p	400.0
Seaperfect	IO & PL @ 120p	25.0
Servisair	IO & PL @ 135p	32.6
TBI	IO & PL @ 33p	26.0
TeleWest Communications[1]	IO & PL @ 182p	393.1
TLG	IO & PL @ 115p	90.0
UK Estates	IO & PL @ 25.75p	9.0
United Industries	IO & PL @ 15p	28.0
VCI	IO & PL @ 150p	31.5
Videologic[4]	IO & PL @ 45p	61.5
Wainhomes	IO & PL @ 170p	41.8
Wellman	IO & PL @ 36p	32.0
Wyefield Group	IO & PL @ 36p	8.0
(USM) London Clubs	IO & PL @ 200p	32.7
(USM) Regal Hotels	IO & PL @ 1.75p	11.0

Source: London Stock Exchange

Key O/S: Offer for sale
    O/Sub: Offer for subscription
    IO: Intermediaries offer (inc. offer for sale in some cases)
    PL: Placing

Notes [1] Pulled once
[2] Profits warning later
[3] Taken over
[4] Demerger

clients with the results of privatization issues. While producing a large shareholder base by introducing a considerable number of new investors to the stock market was a political aim of earlier privatizations, the small size of allocations which resulted from heavy oversubscription often made the holdings uneconomic after dealing costs were taken into account.

Holdings of a small number of shares were considered unattractive for more sophisticated private clients accustomed to investing large amounts. From the point of view of the broker, the huge back office required to process large numbers of small deals was uneconomic if used only a few times a year. The net result of this was that, even taking into account the huge first day premiums and subsequent outperformance of earlier privatization issues, larger clients and certain broking firms declined to involve themselves in mass market share issues. This resulted in a ready market for share issues being denied to the issuing houses.

The consequence of this was the development of the intermediaries offer, in which certain broking firms are effectively allowed to participate in the institutional offer on behalf of their larger clients, and in some cases manage allocations themselves.

The advantage to clients is that they can apply for an economic amount of stock, and also receive better guidance from their broker as to the level of likely allocations. A further advantage is that as a broker will know the level of allocation to each client, it is possible if desired to sell the stock from the first day of dealings, rather than waiting for up to two weeks for allotment letters to arrive in the post.

Stockbrokers also benefit in that valued clients (i.e. the bigger dealers) are separated from the mass of smaller business which most are not set up to handle. A further bonus in many issues is that a commission to the broker of around 1 per cent, but sometimes as high as 4 per cent, can be payable on allocations in the intermediaries offer.

Issuing houses are attracted to the intermediaries offer as it allows access to an otherwise untapped market. The first intermediaries offer was instituted with the BT3 offer and has since been extended to other mass market offers as well as privatizations. In recent international issues up to 25 per cent of the stock intended for UK investors has been reserved for the intermediaries offer.

In the case of smaller offers the shares must be allocated to at least 100 clients by the intermediaries. If less than ten intermediaries apply for shares in the offer all must be given an allocation. If more than ten apply, at least ten must be given an allocation and any scaling down must be effected pro rata.

To participate in the intermediaries offer it is generally necessary to be a client of the broking firm in advance of the offer as allocations will at times inevitably be reserved for long-standing clients. Furthermore, not all private client stockbrokers participate in the intermediaries offer process.

PLACINGS

A placing involves approaching selected potential investors to solicit interest in an issue, rather than inviting applications from the world at large. Placings are often the most favoured method of bringing a company to the market as they avoid the need to involve the general public, more often than not considered a nuisance by investment professionals, and allow the placing broker to select the initial shareholder profile. The most common arrangement is either a straight placing or placing combined with an intermediaries offer or offer for sale.

Under current Stock Exchange rules a stock may be brought to the market solely via a placing if under £25m is raised in the issue. Any issue of between £25m and £50m must involve an offer for sale element, in which at least 25 per cent of the offer has to be marketed via an offer for sale advertised to the general public, or an intermediaries offer, at the placing price. New rules likely to come into effect in January 1996 look set to abolish these requirements.

A placing must have at least 100 places, with fund managers managing several funds considered to be a single placee. In the case of a placing which is combined with an offer for sale or subscription, up to 50 per cent of the stock can be placed firm (i.e. not subject to clawback) with clients of the sponsor and securities houses associated with it. A placing with clawback is a form of underwriting whereby the placees do not hold the stock firm but give it back should there be sufficient demand by other investors.

The majority of new issues which have come to the UK market in the last few years have had a placing element, either with institutional or private client shareholders.

A placing differs from an introduction in that new money is usually raised for the company and existing shareholders may be selling some of their stock. Both new stock raising money for the company and the shares of existing shareholders are placed with clients of the sponsoring broker.

Considerably fewer costs are incurred with a placing of stock, although full listing particulars have to be prepared, and the sponsoring broker does not have to conform to the rigid timetable which a public offer imposes. The great advantage in a weak market is that the issue can be either 'pulled' or scaled down, or increased if sentiment proves to be better than anticipated.

Placings are arranged on an informal basis. The sponsoring stockbroking firm simply tests the water by approaching its clients, both institutional and private if desired, to ascertain their interest in taking the stock. When interest has been firmed up the placing goes ahead and dealings commence very soon thereafter.

Private investors have a justifiable concern that they almost never get to hear of these issues until after the event and even if they want to be involved, the broker is under no obligation to offer them stock. In a placing, allocations of stock are solely at the discretion of the placing broker with no right to fair or pro rata allocations or any right

> **Fewer costs are incurred with a placing of stock**

of appeal. However, brokers will not want to irritate choice clients who might then take their business elsewhere.

Sponsoring brokers would reply that not all stocks are 'appropriate' (a term specified by the regulatory authority, the SFA) for all private clients due to the risk factor, and that the cost of offering the stock in smaller companies to the general public would be prohibitive.

The chances of the private client getting involved in a placing of stock depend entirely on the type of firm involved. One of the top 30 institutional broking firms almost certainly has enough fund manager clients to place the stock successfully without resorting to private clients. The only smaller investors who will see the stock are those who invest in the funds managed by the investment management arm of the broker concerned, or those more substantial private clients whose investments are managed by one of the larger firms.

Conversely, the private investor has a much better chance of seeing some stock in a small issue managed by a less well-known broking firm. There are two reasons for this. Firstly, the vast majority of institutional business in the UK market is handled by the top 30 firms. A smaller broking firm has a large credibility gap when dealing with the larger institutions, and may well not be 'on the list' of approved firms which the institution deals with.

The other reason is simply the size of the issue. Many institutions set a lower limit on the market capitalization of the companies in which they will invest, consigning the others (often with a market value in excess of £50m) to smaller company funds. But the main reason for institutional lack of interest in smaller new issues is the small size of allocations. Even a moderate sized unit trust will generally want an allocation of £250,000 of stock to consider it worthwhile, although it will sometimes accept a smaller allotment to stag the issue for a short-term profit.

This is obviously not in the interest of the sponsoring broker, which would like to ensure a stable aftermarket for the stock and a stable institutional shareholder base.

Smaller placings are therefore structured to allow a handful of larger funds to get their hands on substantial allocations of stock, often several per cent of the company each, with the balance being made up of private client holders. Some smaller broking firms only have a few institutional clients anyway. The great advantage of private clients being involved is that they provide liquidity in the aftermarket.

This method of bringing a company to the market is increasingly being used with 4.2 issues, and is likely to be used with the Alternative Investment Market (AIM), which are both becoming the domain of the smaller broking firms. While they do not have the placing power of a larger firm, companies realize the business is more valuable to smaller firms and they are likely to market the issue aggressively to their better private clients. Whether these smaller firms can keep their companies as clients in the longer term after the company has grown is another matter, as greater placing power eventually becomes necessary.

Placings in the UK in 1994

Company	Price	Raised (£m)
Amey	161p	13.0
Applied Distribution	135p	23.3
Asset Management Inv Co	100p	5.0
Automotive Precision	100p	10.2
Berkeley Business Group	7p	10.0
Bloomsbury Publishing	105p	5.5
Brewin Dolphin	150p	10.9
Brightstone Properties	125p	8.6
Broadcastle	24p	1.9
Capitol Group	125p	4.0
Carlisle Group	20.25p	15.3
Cassell	143p	8.9
Cedardata	105p	14.4
Cementone	73p	4.6
Chesterton International	100p	20.6
Chime Communications	34p	6.5
Churchill China	280p	7.5
Clinical Computing	124p	5.0
Clydeport	133p	23.8
Coda	235p	25.0
Compel	125p	8.3
CPL Aromas	150p	6.3
DCC	Ir 250p	8.1
Dominion Energy	11p	1.6
Domnick Hunter	200p	20.9
DRS Data[1]	110p	15.0
Embassy Property	1p	16.5
Energy Capital Inv Co	500p	90.0
Ennemix	63p	5.3
Enviromed[1]	125p	11.3
Euclidian	100p	20.0
Eurovein	141p	14.2
Filtronic Comtek[2]	105p	25.0
Finelist	130p	15.9
Freeport Leisure	65p	4.7
Games Workshop	115p	12.0
Go-Ahead Group	120p	21.0
Groupe Chez Gérard	112.5p	14.6

Placings in the UK in 1994 *continued*

Company	Price	Raised (£m)
GRT Bus[3]	160p	21.9
Hill Hire	94p	13.3
Hydro International	80p	3.7
IAF Group	33p	3.23
Ideal Hardware	225p	16.8
Independent Parts	112p	8.0
JBA Holdings	160p	19.0
JJB Sports	215p	22.6
John Mansfield	3p	1.6
Kays Foods	5p	2.5
Kiln Capital	100p	25.5
London Securities	150p	1.3
M.A.I.D.	110p	12.7
M.Y. Holdings	52p	11.6
MICE Group	3p	2.5
My Kinda Town	10p	15.5
Newport Holdings	100p	5.0
Nightfreight	105p	17.0
Norcor	120p	17.0
Oxford Molecular	80p	10.0
Panther Securities	90p	1.8
Parkside International	110p	12.2
Persona Group	160p	13.4
Prior	4.5p	4.9
Rackwood Mineral	40p	3.7
Radstone Technology	125p	12.5
RAP Group	142p	6.1
Residential Property Trust	100p	2.0
RM[3]	175p	6.6
Robert Wiseman Dairies	100p	16.1
Roxspur	21p	5.4
Rugby Estates	115p	15.2
Ryland	80p	8.7
Slimma	120p	5.5
Smith (James) Estates	125p	12.8
Spargo Consulting	95p	11.9
Speciality Shops	130p	12.6
St James Beach Hotels	120p	7.8

Placings in the UK in 1994 *continued*

Company	Price	Raised (£m)
Sunleigh	6p	19.3
Superscrape VR	198p	3.5
TeleCine Cell Group	170p	8.0
Trafficmaster	130p	9.8
Trifast	200p	15.7
Tring[4]	118p	25.0
Unipalm	100p	6.9
United Carriers[1]	153p	23.0
Universal Ceramic	86p	6.8
UPF Group	108p	19.3
Utility Cable	10p	4.8
Vymura	150p	24.0
Waste Recycling	50p	5.0
Wellington Holdings	203p	24.9
Wellington Underwriting	100p	17.3
Yates Brothers Wine Lodges	140p	9.8

Source: London Stock Exchange

Notes [1] Profits warning   [3] Bid made or approached
      [2] Price reduced   [4] Float delayed

INTRODUCTION

An introduction is the simplest means by which a company can come to the market as no new money is raised for the company and existing shareholders are not selling stock. However, the fact that an introduction has been arranged and the cost of listing particulars incurred means that either a cash raising will be announced soon or some of the existing holders will sell out. Otherwise there would be no liquidity in the market for the shares and having a quote would be worthless.

All the sponsoring broker has to do is prepare listing particulars and the shares start trading on the specified date. Introductions are relatively rare as parties to the issue would not normally be able to pass up the chance to raise some money.

In an introduction the company has to prove to the Stock Exchange that the securities are sufficiently widely held for there to be some marketability in the stock once trading starts. There also has to be no pre-existing intention by holders to dispose of 'a material number' of shares.

Introductions in 1994

Company	Market Capitalization (£m)
Artesian Estates	9.6
CAMAS (demerger)	238.0
Chester Water	21.0
Dee Valley Water	33.1
Dwyer Estates	25.9
Harmony Property	14.8
New London	8.8
Property Trust (PVT)	10.4
Secure Retirement	5.3
South Country Homes	1.1

TIMETABLES

Offer for sale

An offer for sale is first pre-marketed to institutions on an informal basis to gauge the level of interest and the price investors would be prepared to pay. At this stage the institutions, of whom the top few dozen comprise most of the investment funds in the UK, usually close ranks in what has become a ritual of trying to force down the price expectations of the brokers concerned. All parties concerned are wise to this. The process and the intention to bring an issue to the market is often selectively leaked to the press, along with indications of the expected price range, to gauge wider market reaction and begin the marketing process.

Large-scale issues are then advertised to the general public via television advertising campaigns. At this stage in large-scale public offers for sale, and increasingly in smaller issues, private investors are invited to register their interest via telephone hotlines. This builds up a mailing list of potential investors to add to the list which has probably been purchased. It is generally the case that investors in privatization issues will receive a mailshot for subsequent issues.

The marketing of an issue commences in earnest with the publication of the pathfinder prospectus. This contains almost all the text of the full prospectus for the issue, on the basis of which investors make their decision. However, it does not contain any details of pricing, nor certain other financial information. Note that on occasion substantial changes can occur between the pathfinder and the full prospectus. Very few people in the market actually read prospectuses in full, but bear in mind this is a case of *caveat emptor*.

The company then embarks upon a roadshow of presentations to institutions (on a one-to-one basis with the larger ones) to sell the issue. This can be a global operation in some cases. Increasingly the issue is marketed to intermediaries also, who can then brief their clients. Analysts at the larger broking firms produce research notes giving their opinions and forecasts for the stock in question, a process which continues until applications are in.

Brokers involved in the issue cannot make forecasts in their research publications over and above anything mentioned in the prospectus. In many of the very large issues it is difficult to find one of the large firms which is not involved in some way, which might be interpreted by conspiracy theorists as an effective way of controlling the information flow to the market. In these cases the view of the handful of truly independent well-known analysts come to be of great importance, but bear in mind that there could be an element of spite in some of the more lukewarm comments from those whose houses have not been selected to market the issue.

Publication of the full prospectus and price announcement is known as 'impact day'. The day on which dealings are to commence is also firmed up. Applications are generally accepted thereafter for a period of up to two weeks, but this period can sometimes be as short as only a few days. Announcement of the level of subscription and allocations of stock come a few days later.

The level of subscription and oversubscription is always of great interest to the investing public and institutions as it has a bearing on the likely opening price. However, it is not the general level of oversubscription which is important but the extent to which institutions have got what they applied for (this is often difficult to determine because of the lack of information). The general public are always net sellers in the aftermarket of new issues. Institutions will be buyers of stock in the aftermarket up to the price level they believe the stock is worth.

Before dealings commence, buyers in the institutional and intermediaries offers are informed by the sponsor of the stock they have been allocated. Applicants in the public offer have to wait for the despatch of allotment letters which usually takes place over the next few days, crucially denying them the ability to participate in the first few days of dealing. This is the time when stock can be short and the best prices are paid by some institutions desperate to top up their holdings. However, the institutions are of course wise to this artificial situation and are often content to sit on their hands for a few days to wait for the flood of small private sellers before picking up stock.

Dealings almost always commence in allotment letter form.

Dealings almost always commence in allotment letter form – i.e. the possession of an allotment letter is taken as evidence of ownership of the shares, as it takes several months for all of the allocations to be entered on the company's share register. It is also well known that there is always heavy trading in a large new issue and the company waits for its shareholder base to settle down before issuing share certificates, usually some months afterwards. When dealing in allotment letter form it is possible to sell part of a holding. In this case the allotment letter is surrendered and another one for the balance of the shares not sold is issued.

Placings

With a placing the timetable is much faster and less formalized. Pathfinder and full prospectuses are still issued but the process is speeded up by not having to stick to a public offer timetable. In placings where the only buyers of the stock are large institutions, the application process and announcement of allocations are conducted through the sales staff of the sponsor with almost all telephone conversations recorded. Paperwork then follows afterwards.

The offer period is more flexible as the sponsor can at any time close the books if full, or extend the period. One of the difficulties for smaller private investors is that the whole deal can be done and dusted before the market at large has heard about it. However, an advantage for investors is that with a shorter offer period there is less scope for a market setback between applications and first dealings.

THE US IPO PROCESS

The IPO (Initial Public Offering) market works on an entirely different basis from the UK new issues market, although changes in the pipeline are set to make the two markets more similar. There is no level playing field in the US, and obtaining stock in an IPO depends on the clients' relationship with their broker.

There is no equivalent of the offer for sale where applications are invited from the general public. Instead the process is analogous to a placing and intermediaries offer in the UK, where the brokers to the issue solicit interest from their clients and have sole discretion over allocations. It is important to note that at the stage at which interest is expressed the eventual price of the issue is not known to the investor.

There are so many new issues on the various markets in the US (NYSE, NASDAQ, Amex etc), that no individual investor could hope to assess each one individually. Merrill Lynch alone, the largest broker in the world, introduces as many as five new issues each day in the US at peak times and places them through a network of some 12,500 brokers. As many as 20 issues might come to the market each day on the combined US markets.

Moreover, selectivity is actively discouraged by brokers, and investors are expected to take the rough with the smooth – relying on the fact that the issuing house will support the price of the poorer new issues in the aftermarket. Investors in US IPOs who attempt to go only for the more attractive issues and decline the others will soon find that they are never allocated any stock when a good one comes along.

'Red Herrings'

The IPO process commences with the issue of a preliminary prospectus, (known as a 'Red Herring', for the requirement to give certain information in red on the cover of the document), followed by a final prospectus. Even fewer prospectuses are read in the US than in the UK, given that the brokers encourage investors to go for everything anyway. It is common as in other markets for the issue to come in two tranches: a domestic and an international offer.

Prices indicated

The prospectus will indicate a price range for the issue on the cover, in the form 'It is currently estimated that the initial public offering price per share will be xx to xx', and will also indicate the likely size of the issue. But both price and size can be changed right up to the last minute. The popular Oakley issue was initially indicated at 18 to 20 dollars, but was ultimately priced at 23 after strong interest was shown.

Green Shoes and price support

Should after market demand prove to be stronger than anticipated a 'Green Shoe' option (referred to in the prospectus as the under-writers' over-allotment option) can be exercised to allocate more stock. Support of the share price by the brokers to the issue – known as stabilization in the UK market – is also commonplace in the event that aftermarket trading for the stock is disappointing.

Stags are penalised

Obvious staggs (short term sellers) are penalised in the offer process by being denied stock in later IPOs, as it is of course in the interest of the issuing house to maintain a stable shareholder base.

Allocations and paying for the stock

Allocations of stock depend entirely on the relationship between broker and client, so it is not possible to estimate in any given case what allocations will be. However, it is unusual for even 30 per cent of the interest expressed to be satisfied, and sometimes allocations are as low as 1 per cent. In these cases only the most favoured clients will get any stock. Investors are therefore not required to put up funds to cover their expressed interest, but are required to actually pay for stock they receive. It is not possible to 'flip' a holding (sell in the market soon after trading starts) before having to pay for it.

CHECKLIST

What type of issue is it? An offer for sale is now usual only in larger issues. A placing, often combined with an intermediaries offer, is the preferred route.

Offer for sale

i   *Are there discounts in the public element of the offer for sale compared with the institutional price, or shareholder incentives for long-term holders? If so, go for them, but bear in mind that in an issue of this kind the incentives usually apply only for small amounts of stock, which is all you are likely to get anyway.*

ii *Is it a highly publicized flotation? If so, oversubscription is likely and significant scaling down may occur. Apply for more stock than you want if you can take the risk of getting it all, but bear in mind lost interest income in the money committed.*

iii *What is the timing? Is there a long period between the close of applications and dealings (which increases market risk). When do applicants receive allotment letters through the post? It may not be possible to deal in the first few days.*

iv *Is it a fixed price offer or tender? Fixed price offers have greater potential for first day premiums, but there is a downside as well. Will there be stabilization or a Green Shoe (both intended to avoid soaring first day prices)?*

v *Are any brokers offering cheap dealing facilities and batching of family orders?*

vi *Check rules for applications by other members of the family and for those under 18. Is it possible to apply in both the public offer and the intermediaries offer? Are there special rules for PEP allocations (these may be favoured)?*

vii *Is it part paid? This may increase the attractiveness of the issue.*

viii *Check where applications can be handed in and if possible apply at the last minute. Follow the rules on completing the forms to the letter, and also those for payment. Nobody will check with you for clarification if something is missing; your application will simply be unfulfilled. If you post it, leave enough time for it to get there.*

ix *Do you want to gear up to pay for the issue? This increases the risks as well as potential rewards.*

Intermediaries offer

i *If you want a decent amount of stock, the intermediaries offer may be better than the public offer, but shareholder incentives rarely apply and so you pay the institutional offer price.*

ii *It is usually easier to deal early on as the broker handling your application will be informed immediately about allocations.*

iii *Not all brokers participate in the intermediaries offer.*

iv *Are there incentives to apply early?*

Placings

i) *It can be difficult to get in on placings unless you are already a client of the firms involved. Even then first choice is given to better customers. If you are offered stock unexpectedly it might be that it is difficult to get the issue away.*

ii   *Bear in mind that the timetable for placings is not so fixed as in other types of issue; dealings can commence very soon after applications have been received.*

US IPOs

i   *Bear in mind the relationship with the broker is crucial.*

ii   *Big broking firms have greater placing capacity.*

iii   *Express interest early – it is more likely to be satisfied.*

iv   *The lead house on an issue will give most of any good issue to its own clients.*

v   *Stagging is frowned upon – but does happen.*

vi   *It is unusual to get as much as you apply for – unless it is a bad one!*

vii   *Remember – while investors are encouraged to go for everything you can pull your application if you don't like it at the last minute.*

'The vast majority of market newcomers . . . have made a successful debut.'

3

HOW TO SPOT A GOOD NEW ISSUE

- New issues outperform . . .
- . . . But not all of them
- Growth markets, products and brand names
- Management
- P/E ratios and valuations
- Yield, dividend cover and partly paid stocks
- Takeover targets?

'WHEN TO FILL YOUR BOOTS'

While there have been some high profile disasters in the new issues market of late, the vast majority of market newcomers of the last two years have made a successful debut, and there have of course been some stars. In fact, despite the highly publicized failures, a study by stockbrokers James Capel entitled *New Issue Overload* found that a portfolio of new issues did in fact outperform the market.

Conventional new issues outperform

The Capel study found that if companies with a risk warning, i.e. technology or software companies and those which did not give any price/earnings or dividend yield information ('blue sky' issues) were excluded, new issues outperformed significantly.

In aggregate, issues in 1993 and 1994 outperformed the FT-All Share Index by 6.1 per cent and their relative sectors by 12.2 per cent. This compares with underperformance of 17.3 per cent for technology and software issues and 16 per cent for blue sky stocks, both discussed in Chapter 5.

Given the huge numbers of IPOs in the US it is difficult to calculate their performance, but Merrill Lynch, the largest player in the market calculates that if an investor bought all of the Merrill Lynch issues in 1993 and 1994 they would have outperformed the market by several per cent.

Fund managers have a remarkable herd instinct when investing and this is never more obvious than when deciding whether or not to take a new issue. The same applies for brokers and individual investors. Decisions as to the merits of stocks are made collectively as nobody wants to invest in a heavily undersubscribed issue which is likely to underperform for some time

Nearly half lost investors' money in 1993 and 1994

Out of 130 new issues with a market capitalization of £25m or more at flotation examined by James Capel in 1993 and 1994, 60 were trading at less than their issue price by the end of December 1994. This was against a market background where the FT-SE 100 Index fell 10 per cent in 1994 and the FT-A All Share (a better reflection of smaller companies given the usual size on flotation) lost 5 per cent. Even given the market performance, it is evident that stock selection is crucial.

But after such highly publicized failures as Aerostructures Hamble and McDonnell Information Systems, fund managers have become a great deal more circumspect about investing in new issues. Prospectuses are scrutinized in greater detail and investors are less likely to take a stock merely on the reputation of the sponsoring brokers.

So, what do investors look for in a new issue? As with everything in the stock market so much depends on sentiment and the value of any stock is an aggregate of the views of the market as a whole. That said, there are a number of points which can contribute to the reception a new issue sees from the investment community. Briefly, the market is looking for growth potential, good value, impressive management history and yield.

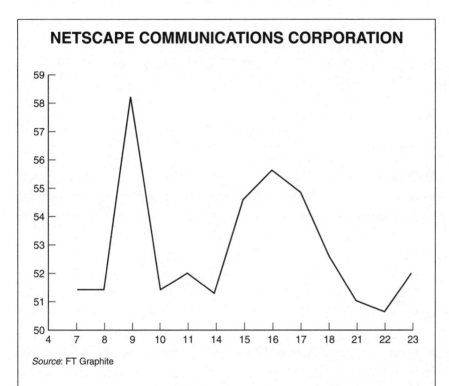

NETSCAPE COMMUNICATIONS CORPORATION

Source: FT Graphite

Surely the most well-known flotation of 1995, Netscape shares nearly trebled on their first day of trading and valued a company founded only 16 months ago at $2.75bn.

At the time of the IPO Netscape had never made a profit and sales in the latest quarter were just 12m. But in a market fascinated by technology stocks, Netscape offered exposure to one of the fastest-growing areas – the Internet.

When the prospectus was originally put together the offering of 3.5 million shares was to be priced at 12 to 14, valuing the company at 500m. This was later upped to 21 to 24, and the issue size to 5.0m, but demand was still strong and the final price set at 28.

Morgan Stanley was said to have buyers for 100m shares even at the increased price, and when the stock started trading (two hours late due to the order imbalance) the price opened at 71 and briefly hit 75. They closed at 48$\frac{1}{2}$.

What is it which distinguishes those stocks which are just barely subscribed from those which cause investors to fall over themselves to get a piece of the action, or to 'fill their boots'. All the best performing new issues have a good story to tell, but the best story of all is the potential for spectacular growth. Guaranteed to get investors excited is the smaller company with a huge potential for growth in its market.

GROWTH MARKETS

Exposure to a growth market is the first bull point likely to generate a very favourable reception for a stock, for it is much easier for a company operating in a growth market to improve profits than for a company operating in a mature market.

Mature (or ex-growth in the terminology of the analyst) markets make for much narrower margins as the players compete aggressively for a share of the action. In a mature market any growth experienced by one player has to come at the expense of another's market share. This leads to price wars, tight margins and slow, if any, profits growth. Look at the experience of the newspaper industry and food retailing. Nobody is likely to launch a new newspaper in the UK any more, and a food retailer could not be floated with an aggressive rating.

Some sectors are perceived as growth markets, notably leisure and some high technology applications. The leisure industry benefits from increasing disposable incomes and leisure time as well as the demographics of the UK with an older and more affluent population (the same demographics also guarantee continued sales for drug stocks, but these are under pricing pressure from the state).

High technology applications are self-evident growth markets, although not always with high margins for the players. But if investors are selective, high tech stocks have produced a higher proportion of stock market stars than any other sector. It is no surprise that several of the best performing new issues of the last couple of years have come from the same industry – mobile telecoms.

While it is also the received wisdom that a smaller company must be able to grow profits faster than a large one – it is easier for a company making $100,000 a year to double profits than it is for AT&T, with profits in the billions – it is also the case that smaller companies often do not have the resources to fully exploit their opportunities. In these situations a link-up with a major partner solves the problem, and for investors the fact that a large company has checked out the product in detail and is prepared to back it is another point in the stock's favour. This is not always the case, however, as the history of Drew Scientific showed..

UNIQUE PRODUCTS

A company with a unique or virtually unique product has a good story to tell, because this means potentially huge growth if there is sufficient demand before competitors can develop a rival. This in turn makes for high margins due to the absence of competition. It

---

TRACKER

Tracker, floated on the Rule 4.2 market in early 1993, soon achieved legendary status amongst followers of smaller companies. Priced at 257 pence when brokers Williams De Broe raised £8m, the shares had hit £16 each by the summer of 1994.

Tracker had only one significant product, but a dream one at that. It had a 15-year licence to sell a US-developed device able to track stolen cars via a radio network. Launched in the States in 1987, 95 per cent of the 5,000 cars fitted with the device were recovered within two hours.

With insurance premiums on the way up, and an affordable price of around 400 pence, the shares had immediate mass-market appeal. But the icing on the cake for Tracker holders was the marketing link-up with the AA (Automobile Association).

The attraction of Tracker for new issue investors was that the product already existed and was proven to work, and in addition had a link-up with a household name.

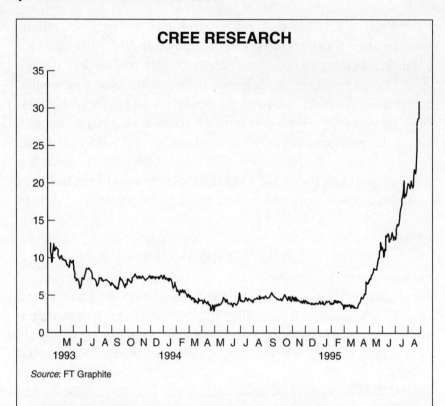

CREE RESEARCH

Source: FT Graphite

Priced at 8¼ at the time of its IPO in February 1993, shares in Cree Research soon tripled in NASDAQ trading to trade at a somewhat optimistic price of 168 times of one analyst's earnings projection at the time of the IPO.

Cree demonstrated the market's love affair with technology stocks, and also had the attraction of a unique product – it made a light emitting diode for computer screens which glowed blue rather than the green or yellow. When combined with the two usual colours, full colour images could be produced.

can of course lead to overdependence on one product with potentially disastrous consequences (see the experience of Drew Scientific) but that is the risk taken with some of these stocks. A monopoly situation cannot be expected to persist for ever, and competition should always be factored in, but if by then the company has established itself as a major player with a substantial market share its subsequent success is all the more likely.

MAGNUM POWER

Source: FT Graphite

Magnum Power was another stock to demonstrate the advantages of a product which technologically less sophisticated investors can easily understand. The company's sole product of note was the Bi-ups built-in uninterruptible power supply for personal computers, invented by the company's founder in 1990.

Investors are generally wary of electronic devices developed by smaller companies – larger competitors can often make up their research and development lag quickly enough and have greater marketing ability.

But Magnum Power convinced investors that it would be close to the break-even point of sales of 6,000 units a month by the end of 1995 – a sufficiently short time horizon. The placing of just 2 million shares at 118 pence was soon insufficient to satisfy demand and an illiquid market later pushed the price up to 195 pence. Magnum Power later warned that its break-even had been pushed back, confirming the fears of the sceptics.

HISTORY

A large proportion of stocks coming to the market are now management buyouts providing an exit for their backers and paying off the debt assumed at the time by the MBO team, so the history of profitability of the company can look decidedly patchy. Often this is a selling point – the story is of a turnaround or recovery. But it is now frequently the case that the company has only achieved profitability in the few months preceding the market listing, and then often only at the operating rather than the pre-tax level because of debt service costs.

Rapid turnarounds look very impressive but can conceal problems, for example, there were allegations that part of the profits growth at Aerostructures Hamble

A genuine profits history is attractive if only for its comparative rarity.

had been achieved by cutting staff, with later disastrous consequences as the skill base of the company was eroded. Questions should also be raised as to how this growth in profitability can be maintained into the future, especially when it has been achieved historically by cutting costs rather than growing sales.

In this respect a genuine profits history is attractive if only for its comparative rarity. Investors have to take less on trust as they can base their valuations of the stock on some historical performance. Of course, as with all investments past performance is no guide to future returns, as financial services advertisements are forced to admit, but in the case of new issues a history of profitability is a comfort factor. It also enables profit forecasts to be more realistically evaluated.

BRAND NAMES

The ownership of recognized brand names is a huge benefit to any company coming to the market, not least because it makes the marketing campaign a great deal easier for the sponsors. The balance sheet valuation of the brands themselves, if any, is less

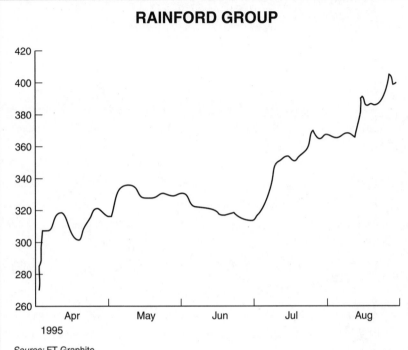

RAINFORD GROUP

Source: FT Graphite

Rainford stood out from the crowd of new issues in early 1995 because it was one of a small number of stocks to join the market which had a consistent history of profitability on which investors could base a decision. It was all the more remarkable for still being run by its founder, after being created in the 1960s. The fact that the company was in a fairly sexy industry – telecoms equipment – also helped, and the issue attracted a great deal of interest. Despite not perhaps being the most exciting of stocks to come to the market, the issue was very well received, rising to a high of 335 pence compared with an issue price of 270 pence, including a first day premium of more than 10 per cent.

important, as this is a contentious issue amongst analysts and accountants. Nevertheless, the City does appreciate the value of brands and the likely long term returns from them. The great advantage of recognized brand names lies in the higher margins they can protect – witness the difference in price between branded

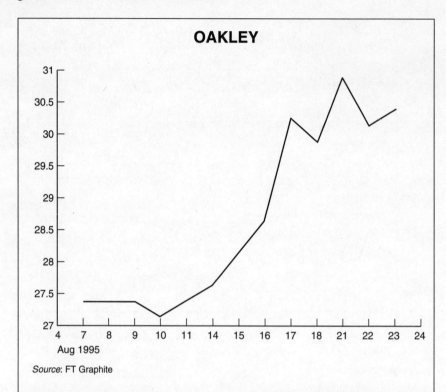

Source: FT Graphite

Oakley Inc was another stock which demonstrated the advantages of a brand name easily recognizable by the general public, especially in a market where the volume of new issues threatens to leave the smaller ones unnoticed by investors.

Oakley (also owner of the Thermonuclear Protection brand) manu-factures a high fashion range of sunglasses, so its stock offering benefited directly from its product marketing.

Expected to be priced in the range 18 to 20, Oakley shares were eventually priced at 23, and still jumped 5 to 28 on its first day of trading.

and own label products in food retailing – and customer loyalty. The marketing term is 'product differentiation'.

Product differentiation applies in the City also – in a new issues market which reached a peak in 1994 of two issues per working day all but the largest fund managers have to be selective as to which issues receive even the most cursory glance. This is even more crucial in the US where an even greater number of issues came to the New York Stock Exchange in 1994. The advantage of a recognized brand name is that institutional or private client sales

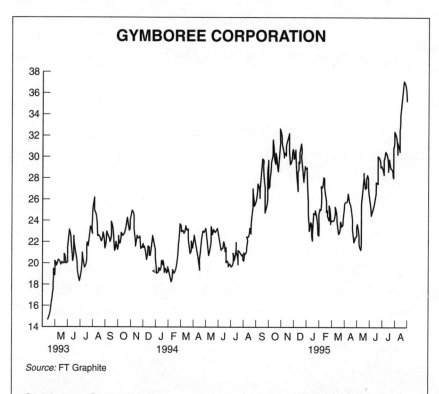

GYMBOREE CORPORATION

Source: FT Graphite

Gymboree Corporation was one of the most popular recent IPOs in 1993, increasing both its offer size and price in response to the heavier than expected demand.

Expected to be priced at 13 to 15, the range was later upped to 19 to 20, and the eventual price at the top end of the range. The offering size was also increased to 2.165 million shares from 1.925. What was the attraction of Gymboree? It was a speciality retailer of clothes and accessories for children up to six years old, not on the fact of it a particularly attractive market. But Gymboree had a product investors could easily identify – it made the multicoloured play balls that children tunnel into in supervised play areas.

staff can more easily attract their clients' attention. The issue is also more likely to attract publicity because journalists are not noted for looking much beyond the first few pages of any prospectus, and brand names offer the opportunity often lacking in financial journalism for a decent picture.

Note that from the point of view of the City a company can have brand names which are widely recognized in its own industry and which are of value, but this is very different from having a brand name known to the general public.

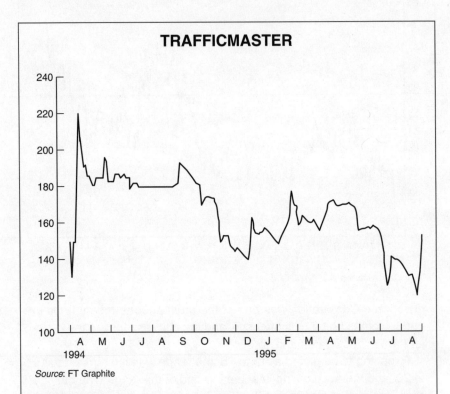

TRAFFICMASTER

Source: FT Graphite

Trafficmaster is a device which allows motorists to avoid traffic jams by having a mobile telecoms based screen in their vehicle which gives real time updates on route congestion. Floated in 1994, a roll-out to the general public was only scheduled for September 1995, but the City could recognize a brand name in the making. The shares were placed at 130 pence but later hit 220 pence.

MANAGEMENT

An axiom of fund management is that institutions invest in people, as the assets of a company are usually of little value if the management does not know how to use them. Therefore the quality of management of a company is often crucial in determining sentiment towards a stock. In addition, many successful players in the equity market make their living by bringing companies to the market and then moving on shortly afterwards, often having arranged a takeover for the company within a few years of its flotation.

> **The quality of management of a company is often crucial in determining sentiment towards a stock.**

These stock market stars can often guarantee a successful flotation for a company merely by virtue of their involvement, although it is fair to say that this happens primarily with smaller issues.

It is difficult to overestimate the importance of management in determining stock market sentiment. The make-up of the board of a company is therefore vitally important (one of the problems encountered by Tring International was that sentiment turned sour when 3i executive Tony Leaver accepted and then turned down the chairmanship.

How long has the management been there?

In general it is a good sign if the same management team has been with the company for several years as it tends to prove that the success of the company and its previous record have not been accidental. However, in many cases the board of a company changes as it gears up for flotation. It should also be said that the type of entrepreneur who is good at creating a company from nothing and building it up is not necessarily the best manager of a company of sufficient size to achieve a market listing. These companies can be run very much as a one-person show in a somewhat autocratic manner which often results in uncertain relations with the City and some suspicion that the company is not being run for the benefit of its shareholders. Those capable of remembering Maxwell Communications can easily understand why the company consistently traded at a discount to the market.

A board gearing up for flotation usually expands by bringing in some additional directors, possibly some non-executive directors, and in some cases a new figurehead chairman. The chairman and chief executive of a company, and their track record, is vital in determining sentiment.

The new issue prospectus should give brief biographies of the directors, from which it should be possible to ascertain how long they have been with the company concerned and what previous jobs they have held. Experience with other public companies is of course a good sign, as is experience of bringing companies to the market.

However, as a large proportion of new issues in the current market are management buy-outs going for a float, the management team will often have been managers of below board level in a larger company and therefore relatively unknown to the market. They will, of course, be introduced to professional investors at a series of presentations known as a road-show before the flotation, but private investors do not have this opportunity. The performance of the management team at these events is watched very closely and can have a significant effect on sentiment.

In these cases the track record of the team since the MBO is crucial, but bear in mind that the team has been backed in most cases by a venture capital firm, which has worked very closely with the board for some years. The reputation of the venture capital fund for picking winners matters here.

In the less frequent case of the management buy in (MBI), the track record of the team both in the company coming to the market and in previous ventures is of even greater importance. This is because MBIs are thought to involve more risk in that the team taking control does not know the business inside out and could encounter some skeletons in the cupboard.

The cynical belief in the City is that MBO teams manufacture underperformance to reduce the value of the business. In the case of an MBI, even more than an MBO, a company coming to the market

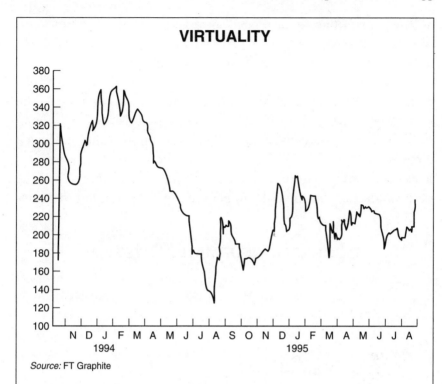

VIRTUALITY

Source: FT Graphite

Virtuality was one issue in the high technology/software sector which did not disappoint investors. Indeed, the advisers to the issue were at the time of flotation trying to keep it low key to stop the share price flying away and subsequently disappointing investors. Nevertheless, the shares ended the first day of dealings 70 per cent higher than the 170 pence issue price.

Virtuality was one of the first companies on the market successfully to develop virtual reality software, a concept at the edge of understanding by many investors. But it applied its software to a market they could understand – computer games – and had associations with the major Japanese games companies.

In a sector which had disappointed so many times, Virtuality came with the reassurance that well-respected venture capital firm, Apax, had backed the issue and retained a significant stake.

only a few months after the buy in (and often for that reason unable to obtain a full share price quotation) might ring some alarm bells. Because of UK Stock Exchange rules on the length of time a management team has to have been on board before a company can receive a full listing, a number of companies in these situations join the 4.2 or AIM markets rather than going for a full quote.

As has been seen in the examples of new issue flops, some concerns have been raised about management buyouts coming to the market very soon after the buyouts, often at considerably inflated prices. It is fair to say that comparisons between the value at which a company was bought out from its parent and the price at which it is later being brought to the market can be meaningless because of the performance of the company in between and the amount of equity

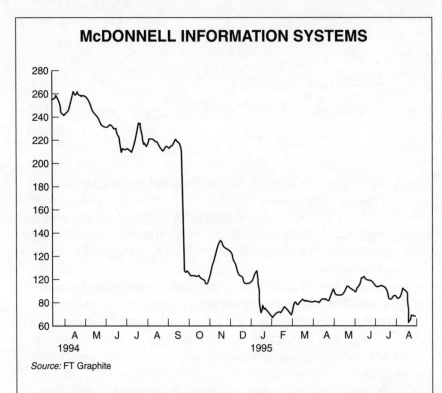

McDONNELL INFORMATION SYSTEMS

Source: FT Graphite

McDonnell Information Systems was bought out from parent McDonnell Douglas for £121m only just over a year before coming to the market in a flotation valuing the company at £250m at its 260 pence offer price. The shares fell to less than half their issue price after the company warned that targets would not be met due to order slippage, and hit a low of 68 pence after a second disappointment.

injected. Nevertheless, spectacular increases in value in a short time can stretch investors' credibility and raise fears that the company is being brought to the market too soon. In these cases it is instructive to see what the directors and their backers are doing in the float.

Management incentives

The management team of most companies coming to the market has an incentive to see both the flotation and subsequent performance of the company succeed for the simple reason that, through ownership of a fairly significant stake, the team benefits on a personal level. Apart from directors' salaries, the other great incentive is the share option scheme, which has come in for its share of criticism in the recent past. Share option schemes are on the face of it a desirable incentive from the viewpoint of the new issue investor. The whole basis of an option is that it only becomes valuable if the company's share price reaches that level within the time period specified (usually two to five years). This gives the management the incentive to produce what every market investor is looking for, namely share price performance.

However, check the prospectus for the size and level of directors' share options. The exercise price of the option scheme is of greatest importance. If it is in the money (i.e. below the flotation price) or only just out of the money, its effectiveness as an incentive is reduced; the option scheme merely serves to add to the wealth of the directors.

Only a scheme which has a fairly high exercise price relative to the flotation price, and can be exercised only in a few years time, serves as a genuine management incentive. It is not difficult to calculate the compound growth in the share price necessary to make the directors' options worth exercising. If this is on a single figure percentage, the growth claims elsewhere in a prospectus could look a little unsupported.

Directors' remuneration

Political views aside, the City as a whole does not care how much the management of a company pays itself so long as benefits are being generated for shareholders – fund managers are far from poorly paid themselves. Salary bills *per se* would only cause concern if they were significant in relation to the profits of the company. However, there has of late been some dispute as to directors' contracts. One major pension fund – PosTel – has openly declared that it is opposed to three-year rolling service contracts for directors and has voted against the re-election of directors at annual general meetings for this reason.

This could have repercussions for the new issues market whereby some institutions refuse to invest in companies which retain three-year (or even two-year) rolling service contracts. The reason they give for this is that a three-year contract gives such favourable compensation for loss of office in the event of the director being sacked that poor performance does not have a penalty.

Are the directors retaining a stake?

There is nothing wrong in the eyes of the market in taking a profit from a successful investment, but that said, sales of large stakes by directors are usually taken as a sign that they at least are not wholeheartedly convinced by their own pronouncements on the prospects for the company in the prospectus.

In the case of a management buyout coming to the market, the directors will often need to sell shares to repay debt incurred at the time of the MBO, but sales of stock over and above this are a negative sign. Most companies coming to the market promise above average growth and therefore investment returns, so the market would not normally expect directors to be taking money out.

One of the most important determinants of sentiment towards new issues is the extent to which directors are retaining a stake in the company. Any large stake sales should be very carefully explained in the prospectus, as should any apparent changes in the amounts to be retained in the run-up to the publication of the full prospectus.

In general the senior management of a smaller company coming to the market is expected to own a stake of several per cent, although this can be diluted with time and further equity raising. This is seen as giving the management a simple incentive as in most cases it will represent the greatest proportion of their wealth.

With larger companies the relationship between management and ownership is not so direct, and the professional management team of a company approaching worth hundreds of millions could not be expected to have a significant stake. However, questions would be asked at pre-flotation roadshows if the board did not have some holding in the company.

Are the original backers selling out?

Venture capital firms sell all or part of their holdings at the time a company goes public, depending on the investment criteria of the fund. However, it is not uncommon for the fund to retain a stake in the company so as to be able to participate in its future performance. Therefore, while it is not unreasonable for the venture capital backers to sell out completely at flotations, it is in many cases unusual and does demonstrate a lack of faith in future prospects.

This is a case of investors wanting a piece of the action, but also wanting to have their hands held by the original backers of the company. However, a small percentage stake retained by the one or more original venture capital backers of a company at the time of flotation is definitely regarded as a sign of good faith and confidence.

P/E RATIOS

The standard measure of value used in most equity markets, although to a lesser extent in some is the price/earnings ratio, otherwise known as the rating. The p/e ratio is calculated by dividing the after-tax earnings of the company by the number of shares in issue to arrive at a value per share. The p/e ratio for the FT-SE 100 index in mid 1994, for example, was just under 14 times on an historic basis.

However, p/e ratios are of little value as an absolute measure. Ratios across the market can vary so widely that comparisons are meaningless, and companies currently reporting losses cannot have a meaningful rating.

The p/e ratio is of value only when comparing similar companies, usually in the same business. Similar businesses are likely to be affected by the same economic and market conditions and, all other things being equal, will have similar growth prospects. The p/e ratio is effectively a measure of the market perception of the earnings growth of a company.

For this reason, *inter alia*, the prospective or forecast p/e ratio of a company, when available, is more important than its historic rating. Company managers are constrained by the regulatory authorities as to when they can make profits forecasts, so most forecasts are made by stockbrokers' analysts.

Regardless of Stock Exchange rules to the contrary, a large number of analysts' profits forecasts are arrived at after a frank discussion with the finance director. From a profits forecast and the price of the stock, a prospective p/e ratio can be calculated. This is usually done for the current and next financial year only, as it is difficult to forecast much further ahead.

Any new issue coming to the market at a significantly higher prospective p/e ratio than similar stocks in its sector has to justify the fact before investors will put up their money. Generally, a high p/e ratio indicates that a great deal of profits and earnings growth is expected from the company in the future.

Companies which are ex-growth in market parlance (cash cows by the classic definition), such as highly regulated utilities or tobacco stocks, will generally trade at relatively low p/e ratios, often in single figures. This usually indicates that the stock has other attractions, such as cash flow, which make p/es inappropriate measures of value. On the other hand a drug company with a proven cure for cancer could be brought to the market even if losses were forecast for several years to come, as the eventual earnings return from the company would be massive.

> A high p/e ratio indicates that a great deal of profits and earnings growth is expected

As p/e ratios are such a significant valuation tool in the UK market, there can be considerable reluctance on the part of investors to invest in a stock which seems to have a too demanding rating, notwithstanding the story it has to tell. This is the subject of exten-

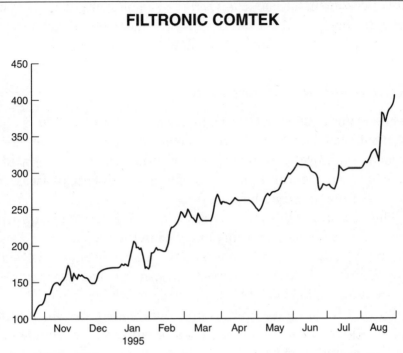

FILTRONIC COMTEK

Source: FT Graphite

Filtronic Comtek was one of the market's surprise performers of 1994, especially after some institutional brinkmanship saw the price scaled back. But in common with other similar situations such as Albright & Wilson, the issue was then perceived as cheap.

The company makes fairly sophisticated base station components for the mobile telephone industry, but the primary reason for the subsequent outperformance was quite down to earth. Even the more technologically challenged members of the City now have mobile phones, and it is always easier to sell something people can understand, and perceive as a growth market.

Moreover, Filtronic was actually making money, and sponsor Panmure Gordon had enough faith in the stock to take some of its fee as a share option. When the valuation was reduced to £44m from some expectations of as high as £60m, investors became interested.

Floated at 105 pence, the price soon rose to 314 pence, making the stock one of the best performing new issues of recent years.

sive discussion in the marketing period of an offer and an element of horse trading with the institutions is often necessary to get a stock away successfully. It is far from unknown to see prices reduced.

Where to find comparative p/e ratios

While historic p/e ratios can be found in the *Financial Times* and even calculated quite easily from the accounts of companies concerned, finding the more appropriate forecast p/es for already quoted companies can be more difficult in the absence of access to analysts from the larger broking firms.

The best sources of information for the UK are *The Estimate Directory*, published monthly and giving the forecasts for most companies covered by analysts, and the quarterly *Hambro Guide*. The *Hambro Guide* is somewhat cheaper but has less detailed information on individual broker's forecasts.

When comparing p/e ratios, sector ratings are generally of little value as sectors can comprise such a broad spread of companies that the average is meaningless. Instead, find the two or three companies in the market with businesses most similar to the newcomer in question. If there is any major difference between the prospective p/e ratios of those quoted and that of the new issue, look for something in the prospectus to justify it.

PROFITS FORECASTS

If a company makes a profits forecast in its prospectus, any claims that are made have to be verified by the merchant bank handling the issue. This is one reason why an issue handled by a larger broking firm with an international reputation might be thought to be less risky than one handled by a smaller broker, although there is no real evidence to support this. Large firms, it is thought, are less intimidated by the companies they are bringing to the market and have reputations to preserve. This has not in fact proved to be the case and some of the biggest flops in the last two years have been handled by the biggest integrated securities houses.

Nevertheless, a profits forecast in a prospectus is viewed as a bull point as it removes the uncertainty of analysts' forecasts, and the company has set itself a specific target to aim for in its first few months as a quoted stock. Recent events have proven all too well that missed profits forecasts are not only highly embarrassing but result in abrupt changes of sentiment towards the stock and its management, as well as sudden share price falls. All of this happened to United Carriers, McDonnell Information Systems and DRS Data. All seriously impair the future growth of the company as investors become increasingly wary of funding future development.

It has been an increasingly common practice in North America for disastrous share price falls to be accompanied some time later by litigation against the advisers of a company for failing to discharge their duties properly and misleading the investment public. Actions have also been brought against the accountancy firms involved with more limited success. It seems likely that such moves could become a more frequent feature in the UK market in the future, and might serve to make due diligence investigations of greater value to the investing public. But the experience of Aerostructures Hamble does not bode well for investors.

Conversely, the absence of a profits forecast in situations where one could have been made is not taken well by the market as it is evidence that the management itself is not confident of the prospects for the company. In very large flotations where most of the large broking firms are involved, their analysts are forbidden from making forecasts. Investors are then very much in the dark as to prospective ratings.

YIELD

The UK stock market has a much greater focus on income than virtually any other major world market. US investors, for example, are much more focused on capital growth. They use bonds to provide the yield elements of their portfolios. US interest rates are also historically lower than in the UK, in the past a more inflation-prone economy. Until the early 1960s and the advent of what was to be known as the 'cult of the equity', institutions did not invest significantly in equities, but had a high proportion of their portfolios in gilts and property. Equities were considered more risky than gilts (there is some logic in this) and therefore were expected to provide a higher yield. The difference in yield between gilts and equities was known as the 'yield gap'. Often equities yielded twice as much as gilts.

However, in the more inflationary times of the latter half of the 20th century it became evident that equities offered one significant advantage over gilts – inflation proofing. In an inflationary economy companies can generally pass price increases through to their customers. This inflates profits and means companies can pay higher dividends. Furthermore, equities in general offer dividend growth if the company is successful and is able to expand profits in real terms.

The outcome of a greater institution focus on the attractions of equities is that there is now a 'reverse yield gap'. The average yield on the FT-SE 100 index at the time of writing was 4.1 per cent, significantly below the 8.0 per cent yielded by long-dated gilts. Historically, equities have often yielded as little as half as much as gilts. The reason for this is dividend growth; over any long period with dividend growth the actual yield in real terms from a portfolio of equities will eventually exceed that of the same amount invested in gilts. Equities also outperform gilts more often than not in terms of total return (i.e. yield plus capital appreciation).

So what does this mean for the new issues market? The consequence of the reverse yield gap is that companies likely to deliver very strong growth, either in capital appreciation or yield, can be floated easily with a below average yield, or none at all. Investors are prepared to wait for their returns, provided the net present value of the returns from the company exceed the flotation price. Companies which cannot promise high growth generally have to pay a dividend yield closer to that of gilts, and there may indeed be some premium to take account of the inherently higher risks of equities, which are not ultimately guaranteed by the Government.

Yield calculations for a stock are made by taking the total net dividend per share (usually paid as an interim and final dividend, but some larger stocks with US listings pay quarterly), grossing up for the basic rate of tax which is currently deducted by the company and paid as advance corporation tax to the Treasury, and

---

NURSING HOME PROPERTIES

Nursing Home Properties came to the Rule 4.2 market in February 1995 having made a number of unique commitments to shareholders. Amongst these was the undertaking to pay out at least 80 per cent of its profits before tax as dividend.

Many companies set themselves dividend cover targets, but few make such firm promises. Other restrictions in the prospectus included limits on management expenses, another bone of contention for some investors.

Nursing Home Properties was unusual in that it existed more by virtue of financial engineering than trading, as its objective was to invest in the burgeoning nursing home market (one 30-bed home is being built every week in the UK) via sale and leaseback transactions. The company was as pure a property investment as one could imagine, but by setting out its dividend targets in advance, investors at least knew what they were getting into.

Institutions came up with the £15m asked of them, but private investors were not impressed and only £1m was raised from them.

---

dividing by the share price to provide a basis of comparison with other equity and fixed interest investments.

PARTLY PAID STOCKS

A partly paid stock is simply one where investors apply for a certain amount of stock in an issue but only have to put up a proportion of the investment at the time of the issue. Further instalments are payable up to two years afterwards, and if these are not made by the due date the right to the stock is forfeited. This happened in the case of several hundred thousand shares in the most recent BT3 offer, even though there is no need for investors to actually put up the funds. The stock can be sold in the market with the call still to pay, at a price reflecting this.

> **The great advantage of partly paid stocks is their gearing effect.**

The great advantage of partly paid stocks is their gearing effect. Investors only have to put up a proportion of the funds but are exposed to all of the benefits (and downside) of the stock. Therefore, if a share valued at 300 pence, with 100 pence partly paid in the first instalment, is viewed by the market as 10 per cent under-valued, it is likely to go up by 30 pence. But a return of 30 pence on 100 is an immediate return of 30 per cent in the short term,

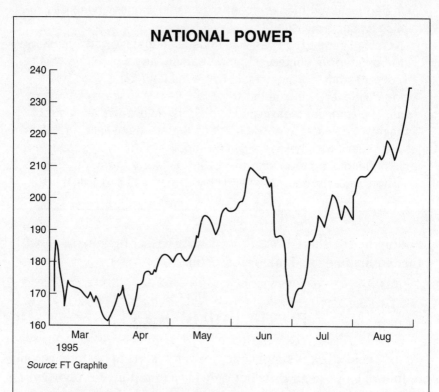

NATIONAL POWER

Source: FT Graphite

The Government's sale of its remaining holding in National Power and PowerGen in early 1995 showed the benefits of a partly paid issue in enhancing an already high yielding stock.

Both companies were operating in highly regulated markets and had in fact been told to reduce their respective shares of the electricity market. This did not mean that profits growth was impossible as both had significant non-regulated businesses, such as involvement with overseas power projects, but it did mean that the stocks could not be sold on their profits growth prospects alone.

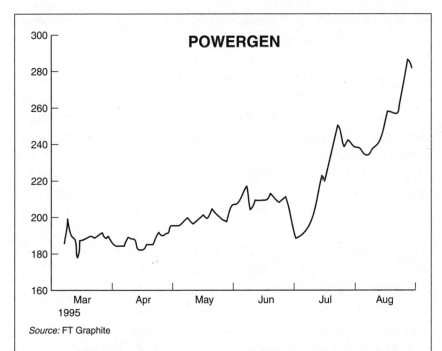

POWERGEN

Source: FT Graphite

In consequence, both companies were high yielders on their fully paid issue prices compared with the market as a whole – with the effect of the part payment they offered gross yields of 7.7 and 6.4 per cent on just the first dividend payable on the partly paid stock. They had also both undertaken to unwind their high levels of dividend cover to provide growth and analysts were forecasting short-term dividend growth in excess of 20 per cent, better than almost anywhere else in the market. To top this, the yield could be enhanced even further when put into a PEP scheme to shelter the income from tax.

before the next call has to be paid. This will be increased by the net present value at current interest rates of not having to put up the balance of the cash.

While institutional investors are not greatly impressed by partly paid stocks as most funds have relatively long-term objectives, and historically partly paid stocks have traded at a small discount to their true value relative to the fully paid equivalent, the gearing offered by partly paid stocks is often very attractive to other buyers. Partly paid issues have been used primarily in privatizations, where it is tacitly assumed that the majority of private investors are potential sellers early on. The attraction of partly paid stock will of course depend on when the next instalment has to be paid and as this time approaches the market will begin to discount the proximity of the next call.

In the Government sale of its remaining 40 per cent holding in National Power and PowerGen, the last of the large UK privatizations, the minimum application was set at £1,000, but as this was partly paid the private investor had only to put up an initial investment of £380.

The other benefit of partly paid stock is the yield advantage, which can often make the investment self financing. A stock yielding 4 per cent gross on its fully paid value, approximately that for the market as a whole and well below interest rates at the time of writing, can yield 12 per cent on the funds invested in year one if only a third of the fully paid price has to be put up at issue. This is because the partly paid stock has a full dividend entitlement. This can be particularly attractive if investors do not have to pay income tax, as when stocks are held in personal equity plans.

There are no particularly compelling reasons from the point of view of the company for making a partly paid issue, apart from attracting investors with the prospect of swift profits. Company treasurers would generally rather have the cash and are able to invest the funds at more advantageous interest rates than the general public.

DIVIDEND COVER

A high yield is only an attraction in a share if the market has confidence that the payout can be maintained. Anything which looks too good to be true is, and if any stock appears to have an historic yield in double figures the general perception is that the company will cut its dividend either partially or completely at the next payout date.

The best indicator of a company's ability to pay its dividend lies in the measure of dividend cover. Most larger companies maintain dividend cover of two to three times, i.e. the dividend is capable of being paid twice or three times over out of the current year's earnings. However, as companies and institutions often like to see a steadily rising or at least maintained dividend – an issue of considerable professional dispute – cyclical businesses will often allow cover to fall to once or even less in the expectation that the situation will subsequently improve.

A company not able to pay its net dividend out of the current year's after tax earnings is said to be paying an uncovered dividend, and is funding the payout from its other reserves and assets. This obviously cannot continue indefinitely as eventually all the assets of the company would have been distributed to shareholders in the form of dividends.

Uncovered dividends are therefore not a good sign in a new issue unless there are some extenuating circumstances. On the whole, companies new to the market can generally get away with lower than average yields as most of them can promise above average growth. Exceptions to this rule of thumb are property and ex-growth stocks, which might have very low dividend cover, as their main attraction to investors lies in the high yield payout.

High dividend cover in a stock which is yielding around the market average is a good sign for two reasons. One is the relative security of the current payout, the other the prospect of dividend growth exceeding profits growth through the reduction of cover, as in the case of the National Power and PowerGen flotation. This level of growth could only be maintained as long as the dividend cover continued to erode, or if profits growth took off – which was thought unlikely in a tightly regulated utility.

Dividend cover is largely irrelevant in a stock which yields substantially less than the market average. In this case the company is implicitly offering the prospect of high profits and capital growth as the reason for investing, although over time consistent dividend growth does mount up.

Another reason why paying uncovered dividends is generally considered a negative sign by the market is that it results in the company paying more tax than it has to. Under UK tax law all dividends have to be paid net of basic rate income tax (currently 20 per cent on dividends). This tax is deducted by the company and paid to the Treasury as advance corporation tax. The amount paid can later be offset against the company's own corporation tax bill (33 per cent for most companies). In other tax jurisdictions similar problems arise due to withholding tax, unless an agreement exists between the company's and the shareholders' tax authorities, known as a 'double taxation agreement'.

ACT is not recoverable in some circumstances, so if a company pays out substantially more than it earns in dividend the payment of ACT can push its tax bill higher than is necessary. This is known as unrelieved ACT, and can also happen with companies which derive a large proportion of their profits from abroad but pay their dividends to UK investors and do not have enough UK profits against which to offset the ACT.

Moves have been made in recent years to take account of this problem with the creation of the foreign income dividend which allows companies in some circumstances to pay dividends out of earnings generated abroad, but ACT remains a thorny issue.

DIVIDEND FORECASTS

Like a profits forecast, a dividend forecast is regarded favourably by potential investors. It is more frequent than a profits forecast and is usually hedged with the caveat that 'except in unforeseen circumstances the directors expect to pay a dividend for the year of x pence net'. There is therefore no binding commitment to actually pay the forecast dividend, but as with profits forecasts, disappointments so soon after coming to the market are not taken well.

Some companies also commit to dividend cover targets, another reassurance for investors that income will be forthcoming and will also grow in proportion to profits.

Forecasting dividends for new issues can be a difficult task as the balance sheet and structure of a company change fundamentally on flotation, especially if the issue is to raise equity with which to pay off debt. Many private companies, especially those funded by venture capitalists, do not pay dividends, but instead reinvest the funds to grow the business. It does not make sense for a cash hungry business to pay its resources out to shareholders and then extend its bank borrowing.

Therefore new issue prospectuses frequently contain the fiction that had the company existed in its new form and paid a dividend last year, 'the directors would have recommended a payout of x pence'. While this is not as concrete as a dividend forecast for the coming year, it does at least give an indication of the likely payout investors can expect in the current year.

ASSET VALUES

A manufacturing company can normally be expected to trade at a premium to the value of its physical assets less debt (the net asset value), if only to reflect the quality of its management and intangible assets of the company such as brand names. However, the NAV per share can be a useful support for share prices, as a company trading at less than its net asset value becomes increasingly attractive to a predator.

Note however that the net asset value is a balance sheet calculation and does not necessarily bear any close relationship to the realizable value of the company's assets or break-up value. Nevertheless, few companies trade at a discount to net asset value. It is important in this respect to check in the accounts to see when the assets of the company, especially properties, were last revalued, and by whom. Independent valuations by property surveyors carry considerably more weight than the opinions of the directors.

PROPERTY STOCKS

For certain companies price earnings ratios are an inappropriate measure of value. Chief amongst these are property stocks and investment trusts (see Chapters 8 and 9). Property stocks generally trade at a discount to their net asset value, to reflect the lack of control over the assets possessed by individual investors. By the same measure, if a takeover were to take place the deal should be done at approximately NAV.

Valuing property stocks can be quite difficult as the NAV fluctuates in certain market conditions, as seen in the early 1990s when values for office, retail and industrial property fell significantly during the period due to a recession-induced drop in demand. Also the discount to net asset value seen in the market varied according to investors' perceptions as to the prospects for the companies and property market as a whole.

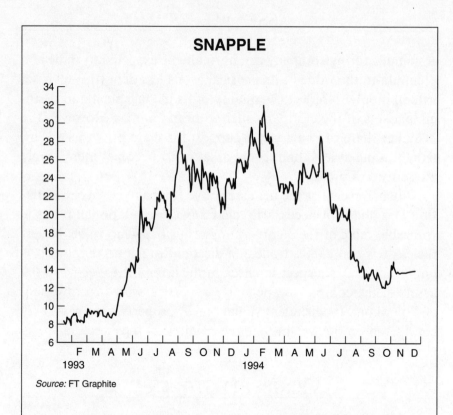

SNAPPLE

Source: FT Graphite

Priced at an equivalent value of 5 per share in the December 1992 IPO, natural fruit drinks maker Snapple shares hit a high of 32 but were only 14 when the company was bid for by Quaker Oats two years later. While Snapple virtually created the market in non-carbonated fruit and tea drinks with 700m in annual sales its cost base was under pressure from defending its market share against Coca-Cola and Pepsi.

TAKEOVER TARGETS

New issues are not normally takeover targets because most management teams bringing a stock to the market have already rejected the cheaper and easier exit via a trade sale. They have invested emotionally in the concept of running a public company. But some make a speciality of listing a company and then soliciting a takeover offer, before looking for another vehicle. In other cases they receive an offer too good to reject and put it to shareholders. In yet other cases a takeover results from poor performance or some disaster afflicting the young and probably small company from which it would struggle to recover.

This occurred in the case of Cantab Pharmaceuticals which had to issue a profits warning when one of its products was found to be no more effective than its placebo in trials. The company's development programme was set back significantly and its share price plummeted immediately to a discount to the placing price. However, the share price improved as the board appointed Lehman Brothers to assist in a strategic review, with a view to possibly seeking an offer for the company.

Investors should not count on a takeover rescuing other bad investments, and in any case the rescue price for such companies would usually be well below the level at which they came to the market.

PARKDEAN LEISURE

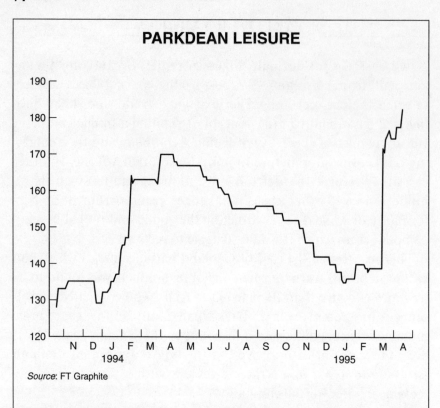

Source: FT Graphite

Floated in 1993, holiday caravan park operator Parkdean Leisure agreed a paper offer from Vardon in February 1995, after less than 18 months on the market, and chief executive Graham Wilson confirmed he had had talks with Vardon even before the float.

Parkdean always looked a little small to operate in the leisure field on its own, and the market float may well have been a way of increasing the price *vis-à-vis* a trade sale after the MBO in 1989.

Whatever the reason, Parkdean investors did well in the end despite the relatively pedestrian performance since flotation. Issued at 120 pence, the shares were taken out with a cash alternative of 162$\frac{1}{2}$ – a decent return of over a third in just over 18 months, but only after a rise of 33 pence on the bid announcement.

CHECKLIST

i   *Is the company operating in a growth market or a mature market? Check carefully, there are lots of sub-sectors.*

ii   *What are margins like? Are they under pressure, rising or falling?*

iii   *Is there a history of profitability to go on, or is it a turnaround? Either can be attractive, but a history can make forecasting easier.*

iv   *Has it got a unique product, or recognized brand names?*

v   *Does it have a larger partner as a backer or associate? Who are the venture capital backers?*

vi   *Does the management have a history of bringing previous successful companies to the market? Are there any 'stars' on the board?*

vii   *How long has the management been there? Is it an MBO or MBI (more risky in the latter case)?*

viii   *Are the management and venture capitalists keeping a significant stake?*

ix   *How much of the sum raised in the flotation is going to the company?*

x   *Is there a profits or dividend forecast? If not, why not?*

xi   *Do historic or forecast profits and/or yields look in line with the rest of the sector? What is dividend cover like?*

xii   *Is there a risk warning? There usually is with high technology, software and 'blue sky' issues.*

'Only invest in something you know about.'

4

WHAT MAKES A BAD NEW ISSUE?

- Management/institutions selling out
- Where is the money going?
- One product/supplier/customer
- What business is the company in?
- Regulatory/political concerns
- Who controls the company?
- Liquidity
- Litigation

A PRICE FOR EVERYTHING

1993 and 1994 saw more turmoil in the new issues market than at any time in its recent history as a significant number of issues were pulled (withdrawn) due to lack of investor interest or inability to achieve a consensus on valuation.

Another high profile group of companies made an ignominious start after coming to the market with a succession of highly embarrassing profits warnings. These included McDonnell Information Systems, Drew Scientific, United Carriers and, most notorious of all, Aerostructures Hamble, where investors lost 80 per cent of their money in just a few weeks.

A recent study by stockbrokers James Capel ('New Issue Overload') focusing on stocks with a market capitalization of over £25m at issue found that nearly half were trading at less than their issue price some months later, and that underperformance was most obvious in the high technology sectors of the market. However, high technology stocks were also amongst the market's best performers.

While there is evidence to suggest that despite the high profile failures the new issues market was perfectly healthy and continued to digest issues at the rate of up to two per working day at its peak in 1994, investors began to scrutinize issues more carefully than in the past. Issues are now pulled more frequently as investors signal their unwillingness to stump up funds under any circumstances, and prices are also being reduced to get issues away. A stock can have a number of undesirable characteristics, but if it is made sufficiently cheap, investors will go for it – in stock market parlance, there is a 'price for everything'.

Cable telecoms stocks are an example of the 'price for everything' philosophy. The UK market does not like cable television as a concept, and many are sceptical of the claims made for its eventual number of subscribers. The same people were, it is fair to say, sceptical of satellite television, but appear to have been proved wrong after the merger of Sky and BSB.

Nevertheless, cable stocks have had a rough ride and after TeleWest only made it to the market on its second attempt, interest in General Cable was lukewarm to say the least. Investors were steered towards a price in the range of 220 to 260 pence, and staged a buying strike. A last minute change of price to 190 secured an oversubscription; those who were unimpressed at 220 pence changed their minds at 190. They should have kept their hands in their pockets – General Cable still opened at a discount, and Nynex CableComms subsequently edged lower.

Albright & Wilson, on the other hand, was a stock which soared to a significant premium after the institutions dragged their heels when the issue was marketed, saying the 200 pence per share price envisaged by US parent Tenneco was too optimistic. Albright, a chemicals company with well-known brand names in its industry, was an otherwise very attractive stock. When the price was reduced to the 150 pence level after the institutional bluff, it soared to a first day premium of 15 pence.

Issues which performed badly, or never even made it to the market, did share some common characteristics. What features are regarded by potential investors as warning signs in a new issue prospectus? Alternatively, what needs to be cheap to be attractive?

MANAGEMENT/INSTITUTIONS SELLING OUT

The biggest danger signal for the market is when those deemed to have the best knowledge of the company's affairs and prospects – i.e. the management team – is selling out in the flotation. This inevitably represents a lack of confidence in the future prospects of the company. However, this is in many respects unfair as it is perfectly reasonable for the founders of a company to realize a proportion of their investment at the time of flotation.

Indeed, in some cases the only way to achieve any liquidity for the stock is for the management to reduce its controlling stake. Where the company has been the subject of a management buyout, the directors often have to sell stock to repay debt taken on at the time of the MBO.

The same reasoning applies to institutional backers of a stock coming to market. Venture capital funds and other backers bring stocks to market to achieve a perfectly reasonable exit and valuation after periods often in excess of five years, but even so wholesale disposal of their holdings is not welcomed.

> **The biggest danger signal for the market is when . . . the management team – is selling out in the flotation.**

However unreasonable this view is, it is nevertheless the case that both the institutional backers and the management team are expected to retain a substantial stake in most new issues to give them a reasonable chance of acceptance by the market at large.

For the same reason that they do not welcome management stake sales, investors are not keen to see the departure of senior members of the management team, especially if they have been instrumental in building up the company. Institutions in particular invest primarily in people, not the underlying assets of the company. In the case of management buy ins, a relatively more unusual occurrence, UK

Stock Exchange rules prevent a company gaining a full listing if the team has been on board for only a short time. The track record of the management buy-in team will be under particular scrutiny.

MANAGEMENT BUYOUTS

Several of the most highly publicized new issue disasters in 1994 – including McDonnell Information Systems and Aerostructures Hamble – were management buyouts coming to the market. In the case of MDIS, the company had only been bought out just over a year before coming to the market. The two subsequent profits warnings in the year following the flotation led to some speculation that the issue had been brought to the market too quickly, or before skeletons in the cupboard had manifested themselves.

Alarm bells are certainly rung when a company can be bought out at a value of xm and come to the market with a value significantly higher just a few months later (but note that the two figures may not be directly comparable if equity is raised to reduce debt). However, MBOs coming to the market after what appears to be only a brief period is now a feature of the market, and a recent survey by stockbrokers James Capel, called *New Issue Overload?*, claims to refute concerns about MBO flotations.

WHERE IS THE MONEY GOING?

Allied with concerns about original shareholders selling out is the question of where the funds raised in the flotation are destined. If substantial shareholders are selling, the bulk of the funds subscribed could not in fact be seen by the company, which therefore benefits little from the flotation.

Other than funds going to the vendors of the issue, it is normal for a flotation to raise funds for the development of the company itself, not least to settle the substantial costs of bringing the company to the market. As with any raising of equity, this exercise goes down much better with potential investors if the prospectus gives

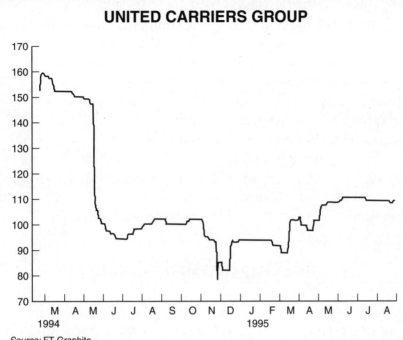

UNITED CARRIERS GROUP

Source: FT Graphite

United Carriers holds the record for the quickest profits warning since flotation, first hitting the market with bad news in May 1994, having been floated at 153 pence in March. The prospectus said the directors 'viewed the group's prospects for the year ahead with confidence', which seemed misplaced as parcel volume fell 5 per cent in April.

Having warned earlier in the year that volumes were too low, the company then warned in November that revised forecasts would not be met because volumes had been too high and extra vehicles and staff had to be brought in quickly to clear the backlog.

By November United Carriers' shares were 79 pence, just over half the flotation price. Institutional investors were said to be sad rather than angry.

With hindsight, could this have been anticipated? Probably not, as other quoted parcels companies, including NFC, were not reporting any difficulties. The only cause for concern was the relatively hefty selling of shares by existing holders in the issue, some 10 million out of the 34 million in issue after the float. United Carriers was bought out from Bunzl in 1989 – possibly an example of the pressure an MBO team can be under to achieve an exit within a few years.

details as to where the funds raised are to be used, for example for acquisitions or development of the company, rather than stating non-specific purposes like working capital or reduction of debt.

Reduction of debt is a perfectly reasonable use of funds for a company which may have used debt funding for expansion when equity capital was either inappropriate or unavailable. Similarly, expanding companies usually see pressure on working capital requirements. But beware of rescues when companies are seeking to raise a significant amount of money. Swithland Motors was well on the road to flotation when the group abruptly went into receivership. It later turned out that the only way the group could have survived was with a cash injection from the flotation.

IS THE COMPANY ASSUMING DEBT?

While it is usual for companies to reduce debt on flotation, in some cases debts can have been assumed. Most flotations in the recent past have been venture capital backed issues, MBOs and privatizations, but there have been some demergers via a placing or public offer. These have included the House of Fraser issue and Alpha Airports, demerged from the (non-quoted) Al-Fayed operations and (quoted) Forte respectively, and Albright & Wilson demerged from US parent Tenneco.

Both of the first two above parents were at the time considered to be under pressure to reduce debt themselves, so the concern was that the demerged operations would be saddled with high levels of debt on flotation. As it is relatively unusual for a parent to demerge either a fast growing or a highly cash generative subsidiary (both are too useful to continuing operations), the ability of the demerged company to repay this debt quickly is in question, as is potential dividend growth.

Levels of debt can be looked at in detail in the pro-forma balance sheet in the prospectus, but a brief statement of the indebtedness of the company is given on the very first page. Debt in itself is not necessarily a limiting factor in the performance of a company; indeed, studies have shown that provided the returns on a company's investments and trading are higher than the amount it is paying in debt gearing, it is in fact an advantage and the company will expand faster than an ungeared rival. The key to debt is not the level of gearing (calculated as a percentage of debt to shareholders' funds) but the level of interest cover. If a company can only service the interest on its debt once over from its profits (and cash flow), it is vulnerable. Interest cover of five times is very healthy.

WHAT BUSINESS IS THE COMPANY IN?

The market a company operates in, and its positioning, is crucial, as experience has shown that certain types of market are considerably more competitive and volatile than others. Any company which is exposed to a higher than normal degree of market risk is likely to trade on a lower p/e ratio, reflecting poorer quality earnings. The most obvious example of this is the commodities market, where traditionally margins are thin and participants often cannot display a consistent earnings stream, but move from profit to loss in successive years.

Commodity trader E D & F Man had a difficult birth as a public company as investors were concerned over quality of earnings. It

---

NORMANDY AMERICA

Normandy America saw its NASDAQ IPO pulled after one day's trading in August 1995 despite having already scaled back the offering to 7.2 million shares from 8.4.

The price had been left at 25, but the first day of trading saw the price slide to 23$^{1}/_{4}$.

Normandy America had been formed only in April 1994 and was intending to use the proceeds of the share offering to build up a reinsurance business and invest in he equity market.

The company was a classic example of investors being asked to put their money behind one man on the basis of his reputation with the market. When conditions in the market are very good it is possible to get an issue like this away, but when sentiment turns these stocks will always be the most sensitive.

also had a problem in that it came immediately after a number of highly publicized flops. There is, as the saying goes, a price for everything, but even so the stock later traded at a discount to its flotation

Certain types of market are considerably more competitive and volatile than others.

price, hitting a low of 160 pence compared with the 180 pence level at which it came to the market.

Financial markets are also highly volatile and effectively commoditized, not least the money market itself. Exco returned to the market in July 1994 with a value of £215m, but just a few months later was sacking staff as market volume declined.

However, the term commodity market can easily be applied to a great many markets other than physical commodities. In 1994 the flotation of the BAS (Buying and Selling) Group was pulled because the sponsors to the issue could not get it away at a price acceptable to the vendors. BAS was involved in the importation and distribution of consumer goods such as fluffy toys and stationery for sale through newsagent type outlets. Now there was no dispute as to the quality of the management, which had indeed brought another company to the market previously, and at great profit to investors after a takeover.

However, the perception of the investment community was that BAS was involved in a commodity business – there is a multiplicity of fluffy toys in the world. One of the fears voiced by potential institutional investors was that the future of the company's profits depended on the trading abilities of a handful of people, who might see competitors move into their low entry cost business at any time. It is true that most companies depend on the skills of a few people, but in this case it was just a little too evident for most investors.

WHAT MARKET DOES THE COMPANY OPERATE IN?

The identification of high and low entry cost markets is crucial as on it depends how easily competitors can challenge a company's position. A high entry cost market is one where any new entrants have to invest large sums in terms of time and effort as well as cash to establish themselves (c.g. pharmaceuticals), while a low entry cost market requires few physical assets (public relations). Businesses in high entry cost markets are more protected from competition and therefore likely to be able to maintain margins (although the example of the motor industry contradicts this), and consequently their earnings stream.

The level of growth expected in the company's market is also crucial as a number of markets are considered, perhaps unreasonably, as ex-growth in stockmarket parlance. Newspapers are a prime example, as there has been little growth in the number of newspapers sold for some years. Growth in sales has to be poached from competitors, hence the UK newspaper price war of the last two years. It is a truism that nobody wins a price war. Companies in ex-growth markets have to convince the investment community that there are growth prospects to avoid having to trade on a sub-market p/e ratio, which restricts the growth of the company and makes it difficult to issue equity in order to make acquisitions. On the other hand, they can be cash cows and high yielders.

PAYBACK

The UK market is often rightfully accused of having very short-term investment objectives, and this is true where most new issues are concerned. Investors like to see a company in profit, and are generally unhappy with 'jam tomorrow' stocks. Any company expecting investors to wait several years before seeing a return is asking them to take a lot on trust, and has to have a good story to tell to attract them.

This attitude has mellowed to an extent in recent years, but the market has learned to be wary of stocks with a long payback time. The upside of these stocks is that investors are in on the ground floor and returns are potentially massive. Nevertheless, there is a distinct credibility gap with 'jam tomorrow' issues and the likelihood is that profits far into the future will see a larger discount applied to them than the strict mathematics of discounted cash flow would indicate. This has been evident in the treatment of cable television stocks in recent months and stems from the dismal performance of the two biggest 'jam tomorrow' stocks so far floated in the UK – Eurotunnel and Euro Disney (see chapter 6).

ONE-PRODUCT COMPANIES

A fair proportion of the time of the average fund manager is spent in risk management, and this attitude inevitably permeates to investment decisions. No fund manager would hold only one or two stocks in a fund, as generally accepted portfolio theory dictates that this is a concentration of risk. If one of the companies goes under it takes most of the fund with it, so the careful fund manager diversifies the risk, sometimes at the expense of fund performance.

This attitude is applied to individual companies and for this reason investors are wary of companies with substantially only one product – i.e. most of the revenues and/or profits of the stock come from just one product or service. The fear is that if demand for the product dries up or there are difficulties on the supply side, the company is unable to produce. The future of the company is then suddenly under threat, and there is no other business to tide it over. This is not always obvious on the face of it as few companies have just one product.

The prospectus should disclose some details as to which of the company's products generate the most revenue. There are, of course, plenty of stocks which have only one product, such as beer, and are perfectly good investments, but in the absence of other factors the p/e ratio at flotation should incorporate a discount to reflect the greater market risk.

The counter to this argument is that most professional investors run large funds and can apply portfolio theory at a higher level by holding a greater variety of stocks to compensate, if desired. There is also the argument that with one-product companies it is at least easier to form a view as to the prospects of the company.

The concern about one-product companies is most evident in the pharmaceutical industry, where companies often derive the

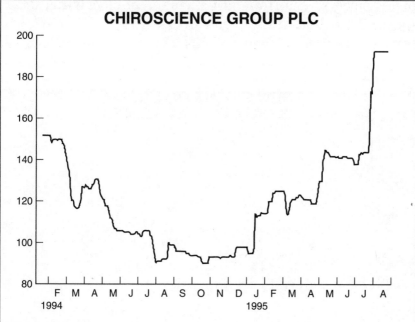

CHIROSCIENCE GROUP PLC

Source: FT Graphite

Chiroscience is the exception which proves the rule, being one case where the institutions were keen buyers of the stock but private investors less than enthusiastic. More than a year after coming to the market the stock was still trading at well below its 150 pence offer price.

The drug stock was no more difficult to understand than most for the lay investor (chiral apparently refers to the isolation of molecules in a pure form to reduce side-effects, and ease of use), but investors were still unimpressed.

Institutions applied for the 16.7 million shares on offer to them with an oversubscription of around three times, but the 13.3 million shares in the public offer received only 10.8 million applications. Why?

Chiroscience came from a good stable – founder Chris Evans had previously floated Celsis successfully and had a decent sponsor in Robert Fleming. But it was a blue sky stock in the extreme. With sales of £2.5m and no profits expected until the end of the century, investors had to take a lot on trust. The final straw seemed to be the increasing of the offer size from £80m to £100m.

The issue also demonstrates the importance of private client money to the market. Private investors often provide the liquidity for smaller stocks and a lot of the buying interest which keeps stocks in the headlines.

bulk of their revenue from just a handful of blockbuster drugs. Indeed Glaxo, one of the largest stocks in the FT-SE 100 index, makes a significant proportion of its revenue from ulcer treatment

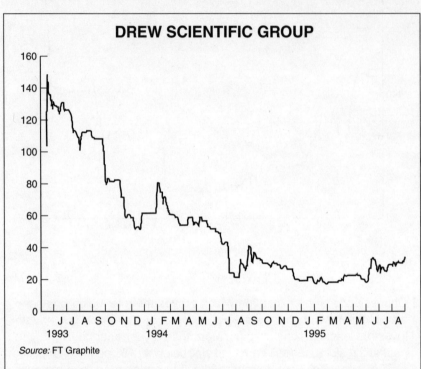

DREW SCIENTIFIC GROUP

Source: FT Graphite

Drew Scientific, through no fault of its own, demonstrated all of the potential problems attendant on scientific research based companies, although this may equally well apply to any small company with few products and even fewer distribution channels.

Drew Scientific was floated in 1993 with a market capitalization of £25m at its launch price of 105 pence. The price dropped to as little as 19 pence after a faulty component was detected in the only product the company produced – a machine to manage diabetes. Its only distributor, Siebe, put a block on shipments and Drew did not make a profit in the two years after flotation.

On the face of it Drew Scientific had two salient attractions to investors: a product involved in the management of a common and chronic illness and an association with a FT-SE 100 company. Neither of these was a help when the company's sole source of revenue was cut off.

Zantac, the world's best-selling drug. When patents expire, generic drug manufacturers can challenge for a part of the market, hitting sales and margins. While most drug companies do not derive all their revenue from a single product, but spend huge amounts on research and development to come up with the next generation, they do have some of the characteristics of one-product companies.

ONE SUPPLIER/CUSTOMER

More serious than a company with one product is that with only one supplier, or even worse, one customer. If supplies are sourced from only one point the company can be at the mercy of margin pressure from price increases, or even a total breakdown of supply. It is rare for there not to be alternative sources of supply, but considerable disruption can be caused to trading if it is necessary to relocate.

A company which derives the bulk of its income from one customer always rings warning bells with investors, as its risk profile is substantially increased. Not only are the earnings of the stock heavily dependent on the performance of another company, but the customer can always desert to a more competitive supplier. Long-term business relationships such as those between Japanese motor manufacturers and suppliers are not a feature of Western business culture, and even the closest relationships are rarely contracted for more than a few years.

The flotation of brewer Ushers was pulled for this reason. An otherwise attractive track record from the MBO team was overshadowed by a beer supply contract with Courage which accounted for a substantial proportion of turnover, and investors were concerned that in an over-supplied beer market Ushers would find it difficult to replace the sales were the contract not to be renewed.

ONCE BITTEN, TWICE SHY

The stock market has had a series of bad experiences with companies in some industries, and memories can be long lived. One of

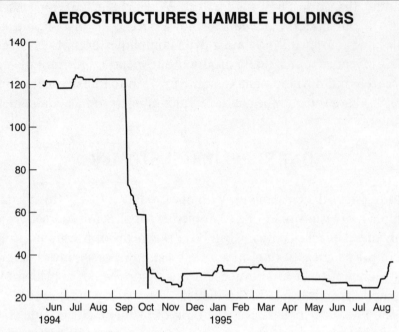

AEROSTRUCTURES HAMBLE HOLDINGS

Source: FT Graphite

Aerostructures Hamble was far and away the most notorious new issue on the UK market in 1994, flopping to a fifth of its flotation price within six months of its float after a profits warning. Aerostructures, bought out from British Aerospace two years earlier, experienced production difficulties in making parts for Harrier jet fighters with disastrous consequences.

Such was the anger amongst investors that one institution was reported to have taken its lawyers along when it went to hear the company's explanation of the fiasco, which also cast doubt on the value of the investigations by the accountants and merchant banks concerned.

Aerostructures' difficulties apparently started four months before the flotation when the company had quality problems with a batch of Harrier aircraft sections for BAe. To cope with any further problems the shop floor was told to produce components for the entire production run, sufficient for two years, and geared up to do so. But then just before the flotation in June, BAe asked Aerostructures to increase production of parts for its Hawk aircraft and the factory seized up as it was unable to deliver, being fully engaged in Harrier production. Orders for future work were subsequently cancelled or delayed.

By November the shares, floated at 120 pence, were 24 pence.

Shareholders were justifiably angry that this had happened in the first place, and that all the advisers to the company had failed to spot it. There were suggestions that the management, which made a substantial sum from the float, took its eye off the ball to concentrate on the onerous task of preparing the prospectus. But what happened with the advisers?

Despite talk of legal action, it seems that nothing will come of the issue and that investers have no real prospect of legal redress against the advisors in fiascos of this kind. But it does raise the question of whether the good name of the sponsor, in this case Rothschild, is of any value to investors.

It would seem that it is not. Investors can seek legal action, and GE Capital did sue the advisers over the Magnet MBO, but it is very rare, and the experience of the flops of the last few years is that investors cannot rely on the law.

Could any of this be spotted in advance? The only clue to any potential disaster in the case of Aerostructures was that it was an MBO from a much larger parent, BAe, which crucially remained the company's largest customer. So Aerostructures was a company with only a handful of products, and dependence on one customer.

Another danger sign might have been the rapid improvement in profitability at the MBO, as there were allegations at the time of the profits warning that in making staff redundant to reduce the cost base, the company had dispensed with critical skills in a high quality business.

these industries is leasing. It would be difficult, if not completely impossible, to float a leasing company in the UK, however attractive its profitability and very difficult in the US after the global GPA float was pulled. The collapse of Atlantic Computers and the pulling of the huge GPA float, and subsequent near collapse of the aircraft leasing firm, would ensure a hostile reaction. Leasing is regarded as financial engineering by many investors, and other issues in the financial sector would be tarred with the same brush.

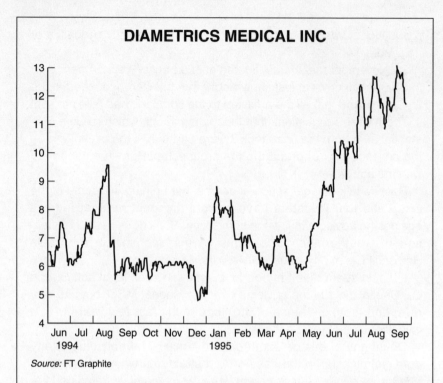

DIAMETRICS MEDICAL INC

Source: FT Graphite

The dramatic impact litigation can have on the new issues market was amply demonstrated by the experience of Diametrics Medical, which had to withdraw its IPO at one point.

Diametrics shares were priced at 13 per share and traded as high as 14³/₄ in the brief period of trading before PPG Industries launched a law suit claiming the company had infringed its patents for the blood gas analysers. Some analysts were reported to have estimated the stock would have halved had the deal gone ahead.

Withdrawal of IPOs after they have been priced happens only a handful of times a year in the US.

LITIGATION

One issue guaranteed to overshadow any flotation is that of litigation. While most large companies are conducting a legal dispute with somebody virtually all the time, and with no ill effects, some legal cases are of fundamental importance, especially to smaller companies. Court actions are worrying, not least because of their length and cost (especially those fought in the US), but also due to the potential effects on the company's ability to carry on its business.

This is especially true of pharmaceutical or technology companies which depend for their existence on the intellectual property contained in a handful of patents. The drugs industry in the US has recently seen the emergence of 'patent busting' actions by generic drug manufacturers keen to break up the monopoly on a new drug conferred by the patent.

> **An ongoing or imminent court case is always a dampener on flotation prospects.**

However confident the company may appear with regard to the outcome of legal actions, the presence of an ongoing or imminent court case is always a dampener on flotation prospects, even if a full provision for costs has already been made.

WHO CONTROLS THE COMPANY?

Who has effective control of a floated company is important because on it depends such things as dividend growth and growth prospects. Private companies have only one or just a handful of shareholders, but publicly quoted companies have to take into account the interests of many shareholders, and in the case of privatized utilities, customers as well.

If a sufficiently large proportion of the shares, and the attendant votes, are held by one party, it effectively controls the company. Under Takeover Panel rules in the UK a holding of 30 per cent is deemed to be effective control, beyond which a full bid has to be made for the company. Effective control could exist with an even smaller holding depending on the shareholder profile. The US SEC (Securities and Exchange Commission) has a notification point at 15 per cent. But a company can easily be floated with a much bigger block held by one party. Smaller companies, particularly on the new AIM market, can float as little as 10 per cent of the equity, leaving other holdings unchanged.

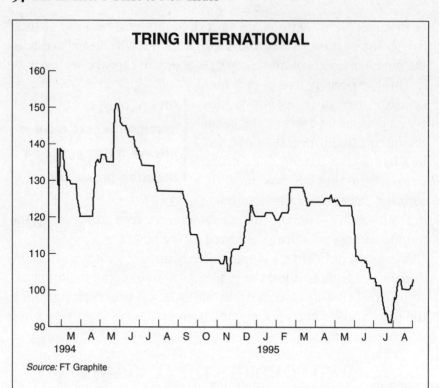

TRING INTERNATIONAL

Source: FT Graphite

Tring's problem was that the market simply could not believe that the company could sell its budget music CDs without infringing somebody else's copyright. And writs from Polygram, MCA and EMI did not help, although they were settled with relatively small payments in the region of £20,000 at the time of the February 1994 float.

A flotation at the end of 1993 was delayed – 'categorically not because of the litigation', according to Tring – and sentiment towards the stock was not helped when former 3i chairman Alan Wheatley withdrew his acceptance of the chairmanship.

The prospectus stated that litigation was not expected to have a significant financial impact on the company profits of around £5.1m and the placing of 49.9 per cent was oversubscribed. But over a year later Tring shares were barely higher than the 118 pence flotation level.

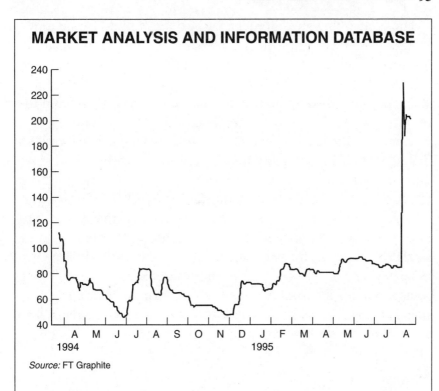

MARKET ANALYSIS AND INFORMATION DATABASE

Source: FT Graphite

M.A.I.D. was another example of market scepticism, as many potential investors found it difficult to believe, despite management
assurances to the contrary, that the vast quantity of data accessible
via the company's database could be achieved without substantially
higher royalty payments.

In the case of very small companies this could be of particular
concern as the management may still treat the company as a private one, giving minority shareholders little say in what goes on.
The primary concern here is over dividend policy and expansion.

Private companies do not often pay returns to shareholders via
dividends as it is not especially tax efficient. The founder of a company, who still retains a 75 per cent stake, could also retain a
private company mentality along with the other directors and be
unwilling to pursue a progressive dividend policy, preferring to
retain funds in the company. Minority investors hoping for yield
growth could do little about it.

The controlling stakeholder in a business could also be unwilling to give up control, which can restrict expansion. If expansion has to be funded by a rights issue, and the controlling party does not have funds to take up its rights, it would suffer dilution of its stake, possibly eroding its control. This could be a significant disincentive to expansion by any method other than organic.

That said, the market generally regards it as a positive sign if the management of a company holds a reasonably substantial stake, and it is not unusual in the case of a demerger for the parent to retain a significant stake in the future performance of its erstwhile subsidiary. However, it does appear to be the case that UK institutions prefer to see a greater than 50 per cent free float in all but the smallest companies for two reasons. Given that institutions control in aggregate some 70 per cent of the equity in the market, it gives some scope for institutions to collectively express their dissatisfaction by using their voting power (albeit a very unusual occurrence), and a company with no controlling stake is always open to a hostile bid should it underperform.

OVERSEAS SHAREHOLDERS

If there is one thing worse than a company controlled by a substantial domestic shareholder, it is one controlled from overseas. Apart from the xenophobia for which the City is well known there are some good reasons for this. Domestic investors have a remarkable consensus as to investment objectives, and this extends to the UK obsession with dividend income. Foreign investors may not have these preoccupations, and in fact may find it more tax efficient to retain funds in the company, jeopardizing dividend growth.

There is also the concern that some companies controlled by foreign investors are vehicles to channel funds out of their domestic markets, which may or may not have consequences for investment policy. The most obvious example of this is the appearance on the share register of a number of small property companies of investors operating out of Hong Kong in advance of 1997.

Control by a substantial foreign shareholder can also affect the treatment of a company by the UK authorities. Waste Management, for instance, has a market capitalization large enough to justify inclusion in the FT-SE 100, but because it is 75 per cent controlled by its US parent, it is excluded. Rentokil, however, has a FT-SE 100 place with a 52 per cent holding by Sophus Berendsen. Finally, the authorities sometimes place restrictions on holdings by foreign investors. British Aerospace has a limit on ownership by non-UK investors of 30 per cent. Should this level be breached, overseas holders can be forced to sell stock.

DIVIDENDS

The UK equity market is unique in the world in its concentration on dividends. Yields in the UK market are much higher than in other major world markets (cited by some as a contributory factor to the under performance of UK quoted companies) and some institutions are keen to see companies pay uncovered dividends in recession to maintain payout levels. It is accepted that growing companies yield less than mature companies and need to retain the funds in the balance sheet to finance expansion, but nevertheless the UK market likes to see dividends and dividend growth.

There is some justification for this – dividends represent real cash and a tangible return, and pension funds need income to pay their pensioners. This concentration on dividends does have one important

Yields in the UK market are higher than in other major world markets.

consequence. Certain fund trustees will not allow investment in companies which do not pay a dividend, which results in some companies paying a nominal 0.1 pence per share dividend. But it does restrict the potential investors in a new issue which does not intend to pay a dividend, and illustrates that interest could be lukewarm in any issue which does not promise either a market average payout or dividend growth to compensate.

IS AN ISSUE BEING HYPED?

One of the most basic investment rules is only to invest in something you know about, a rule broken frequently in the case of technology issues. Very few of the professionals in the stock market have anything but the most superficial knowledge of technology stocks, and are therefore susceptible to any hype surrounding the issue. Alternatively, the issue generates little interest because investors cannot understand the company's products. For a period in 1994 anything involving multimedia – a much abused and widely applied phrase – was chased to unreasonable p/e multiples by excited stockbrokers. The financial press was even running an article on the flotation of The Multimedia Corporation within a few days of the company deciding to go for it, i.e. potentially several months before the issue.

On the face of it, it is difficult to tell whether an issue has generated genuine investor and press interest, or is being hyped by the sponsors and their PR campaigns. However, bear in mind that there are several hundred new issues a year and all other things being equal, most smaller companies will not justify more than a mention in the financial press and the publication of the pathfinder or full prospectus. Beyond that, only stocks with brand names known to the public at large, or those which offer a photo-opportunity, are likely to receive more coverage.

It should also be borne in mind that, despite internal rules to the contrary, financial journalists are often far from the impartial observers they seem and may well be existing holders or applicants for stock in a new issue. It is in their personal financial interest for the issue to go well, especially as most are stags rather than long-term investors. Therefore some suspicions should be raised, especially in the case of very small new issues, if what seems to be an inordinate amount of press coverage is generated.

In the case of larger issues such as privatizations, widespread press coverage is of course to be expected and there is little or no personal incentive on the part of journalists. Nevertheless, the size of any advertising and marketing campaign relative to the total value of the issue is worth considering. All the costs have to be paid for out of the proceeds of the issue, and a television advertising campaign can easily run into the millions. A full page spread in a national newspaper costs tens of thousands of pounds.

Is all this worth it to get an issue away? Consider what proportion of the sum invested in the issue has been spent before the company even gets to the market. Given that for a long time sponsors accepted the necessity of having a public offer element in larger issues only with bad grace, it might be suspected that in some cases issues are offered to the general public in the hope that they will not look too closely at what is on offer. The adage about not wanting to join any old club that would have you as a member applies.

Nevertheless, many if not most public offers with attendant marketing campaigns do go very well, so widespread press coverage and advertising is not necessarily a bad thing. But one aspect of a new issue which always generates disparaging comment amongst investment professionals is the number of advisers involved. This is especially true of international issues, where it can seem that just about every well-known securities house is in on the act. Apart from reflecting some diplomacy on the part of the big houses by letting each other have a piece of the action, the argument is presumably that each house on board improves the placing and marketing power with the institutions. This it does to some extent as the list of institutions is generally carved up between them with the lead sponsor taking the 50 or so most important worldwide.

However, it does raise some concerns about the quality of the issue – anything which has to be sold so heavily, rather than bought on merit, deserves some suspicion. Another potential concern is that being involved with an issue muzzles a firm's analysts, who are prevented from issuing profits forecasts for the company for the duration of the offer process. One issue which had a bevy of advisers was cable television and telecoms operator TeleWest, which despite their firepower had to be pulled at the first attempt, although it was later floated successfully. Leasing group GPA also saw its first full apart at the last minute despite a very aggressive institutional marketing campaign.

Good financial PR firms can also help to get an issue away by focusing attention on the issue through their personal contacts. In

the case of the flotation of BAS Group (later pulled from lack of
interest) journalists were sent a huge box full of the company's
products. While this certainly generated press coverage and attention, it was perhaps counterproductive as it brought home just
what some of the items were!

Advertising campaigns

Television advertising of new issues is treated almost universally
with derision in the City, not least the recent power issue where
none of the sources of energy featured in the campaign was uti-
lized by the two companies up for
sale. Most financial services advertising suffers from the same
problem. The message to be put
across is potentially very complex
and regulatory concerns limit that
message still further. Advertisers
of new issues are effectively limited
to publicizing the closing date

**These campaigns
are mounted at vast
expense, which must
come out of the
proceeds of the share
issue.**

with the implication that the general public is in danger of missing out. This trades on the historic early performance of
privatization issues which were intentionally underpriced and
saw some large stagging profits for investors who had previously
not owned shares.

The British Gas 'Tell Sid' campaign was the high point of new
issue advertising and did at least raise consumer awareness, as
measured by the response of the pressure groups opposed to the
issue (Tell Sid he owns it anyway!). But campaigns of this nature
do raise some concerns with the investment community, as they
demonstrate that the issue is being marketed to people outside the
normal investor base.

Why is this a cause for concern? Is it because the sponsors do
not believe they can get the issue away if marketed solely to institutional and larger private clients? In this case it is a cause for
concern as a large proportion of smaller investors are not stable
long-term holders. These campaigns are also mounted at vast

expense, which must come out of the proceeds of the share issue.

However, Stock Exchange rules require that at least a proportion of any new share issue must be marketed via an offer for sale or subscription, so in most cases the advisers to the issue are simply making a virtue out of necessity. Utilities such as British Gas mount large-scale public awareness campaigns anyway simply to raise the profile of the name with the general public, without any further message. The advertising of share issues achieves the same objective. And the BSkyB issue also fitted in well with the current advertising campaign.

In this respect the 3i (Investors in Industry) 'Jeremy' campaign was a little different. 3i is the largest provider of venture capital to growing firms in the UK, and had already marketed itself heavily before the share issue. For 3i a share issue served a useful purpose in raising the profile of the company with the target group which might one day have need of its products – relatively sophisticated private investors. The selection of the name Jeremy rather than Sid was not made by accident. TV advertising campaigns are not used in the US market, in part because there has not in the past been a political incentive to encourage wider share ownership.

WHY IS THE COMPANY BEING LISTED HERE?

The UK stock market is not known on the whole for supporting aggressive valuations of companies. At the end of 1994 the average historic p/e ratio for the main UK indices was substantially lower than for equivalent US indices. So there is no fundamental reason why a company should choose to list in the UK, different reporting standards notwithstanding. In fact the opposite is true and higher valuations for the same business can often be achieved elsewhere in the world.

However, a number of companies are listed in the UK while all or substantially all of their business is done overseas. There are historical reasons for many of these UK listings, but in the case of a new issue some questions have to be asked. A company will normally only seek a listing in another market if it cannot obtain a listing in its main market. Now the UK, apart from the new AIM market, is also not known for having particularly lax listing standards.

So in the case of any new issue which does not appear to have any real links with the UK, the market will want to know the reason for the desired UK listing and will also be concerned that the geographical remove might be intended to conceal something. It is more difficult to obtain information on a small US company and its competitors from the UK, for instance, than it is to track down a domestic one.

POLITICAL CONCERNS AND LEGISLATION

An example of political concerns affecting investor interest was the situation in the UK in 1995 when opinion polls were indicating the likelihood of a Labour Government and the City was beginning to take its industrial and corporate policy statements seriously as the intentions of the next government. Previously privatized utilities were the most obvious target but the party also committed itself to more stringent corporate governance to regulate directors' pay and possibly the renationalization of British Rail if successfully sold off. Statements such as these from a party possibly only a few years from government would, needless to say, significantly reduce investor interest.

However, a more pressing concern is that of less highly political legislation which could nevertheless significantly impact certain sectors. One of the most obvious of these is European Community legislation on environmental issues such as waste disposal, and eventual possible restrictions on drug pricing, already a feature of some European markets. All such legislation can affect companies, but the rules are uncertain as to how much these risks should be disclosed in a prospectus, especially if it is likely to take effect only a few years hence. Litigation has already arisen in the US with oil and chemicals giant Shell faced with a multi-million dollar law suit for contamination.

REGULATORY CONCERNS

The fallout from the debacle of the National Power and PowerGen flotation clearly illustrated the risks of investing in highly regulated industries where companies are not necessarily allowed to be run in the interests of shareholders. British Rail looks likely to be in a similar position when and if it ever gets to the market, it is possible that a price cap would be put on fares, similar to that imposed by the Government on British Telecom and the water and electricity utilities.

The concern for investors in these companies was amply demonstrated just days after the final sale of the Government's holding in National Power and PowerGen was completed, and the partly paid stock started trading. Office of Electricity Regulation (OFFER) chief Professor Stephen Littlechild announced that as a result of new information coming out of the Trafalgar House bid for Northern Electric, and the potentially huge payouts to shareholders, he was to reconsider the pricing regime for the regional electricity companies. While this had no direct impact on the power generators, the market was immediately concerned at the moving of the goalposts.

It was pointed out that had this review been published just weeks earlier, the price the Government could have got for its £4bn stake in the power generators would have been substantially reduced. There were allegations of insider trading by the Government, and the market was highly sceptical of claims that while the advisers had been informed of the likely review, they thought it not necessary to inform potential investors.

Investors in any other industry likely to be highly regulated should learn their lesson. Such is the political involvement with these issues that these companies are subject to interference at the highest level, to the point where they are not being run entirely for the benefit of shareholders. British Rail will be subject to a regulator and a cap on ticket prices, and Nuclear Electric will also be highly regulated. What will happen if the cost of decommissioning older reactors is suddenly reassessed? Shareholders will pay.

LIQUIDITY

A very low level of free float (i.e. shares held by investors other than management and long-term institutional holders) in a company's shares is certain to produce rapid price gains if large sums of money are chasing the small amount of stock on offer, and can result in healthy premiums in an oversubscribed new issue. But poor liquidity is a double-edged sword and can be very painful on the downside. Sponsors to a new issue make relatively large sums of money from the flotation and hope to be the broker to subsequent rights issues and acquisitions, but in the meantime illiquid smaller companies generate little in the way of commission income.

The danger is that companies which do not display a degree of corporate activity see broking analysts desert them as no money is to be made, which in turn leads to a lack of institutional dealing interest and in some cases to market makers losing interest in the stock. Several stocks lose their full listing each year because little or no business is done in the shares and no market maker is prepared to run a book.

Lacklustre trading makes for small dealing sizes (i.e. the parcels that stock market makers are prepared to deal in without widening their spreads) and wide spreads. The spread between the bid and offer price of a share, effectively the market maker's profit on any deal,

Several stocks lose their full listing each year because little or no business is done in the shares.

is already much wider for smaller company stocks than for FT-SE 100 stocks. A spread of 10 per cent is far from unusual in smaller company shares, whereas for larger ones it could be as little as 1 per cent or even a penny per share.

MARKET MAKERS

Except in the smallest companies and the AIM market, the UK stock market works on a competing market maker system, which usually requires two market makers to each run a book (although their prices can match exactly for much of the time). For larger stocks, market makers are generally falling over each other to make a market and see some of the large-sized institutional trading, albeit at tighter margins, which produces a healthy market and narrow spreads.

The US NASDAQ market is similar to the UK, being 'quote driven', but the NYSE is 'order driven', depending on so-called specialists to match buy and sell orders. With thinly traded stocks the distinction between the two systems becomes very blurred.

But many smaller new issues do have just two market makers. Often one of them will be the market making arm of the integrated securities house whose broking arm has brought the company to the market, and it will be allocated stock, perhaps up to 5 per cent, in the flotation with which to runs its book immediately after the issue, hoping for aftermarket buying interest. This also usually ensures that an analyst from the firm will cover the stock, making periodic profits forecasts and keeping the institutions informed as to what is going on. But many smaller companies are brought to the market by smaller firms which do not make markets on any formal basis.

In these cases they have to find a market maker which will take the company on board. Many smaller stockbroking firms effectively make a market in a number of stocks simply by knowing where the stock is because they sold it in the first place. By doing regular agency cross deals and by running a small market making position of their own, an effective dealing market can be maintained in these companies.

But for around 1,150 smaller companies, one of their two market makers is Winterflood Securities, run by a well-known City character Brian Winterflood, but owned by merchant bank Close Brothers. Winterflood Securities is a simple market maker with no corporate finance arm, and the list of stocks is handled by a dealing team of no more than 30. The implication of this is that the vast majority of the stocks handled by the firm do not see a lot of trade on the average day and also that it is relatively difficult to deal in the smaller companies market.

This is by no means an indictment of Winterflood, which provides a welcome service to the companies, many of which would otherwise be in danger of losing their quote. Trading in these companies tends to perk up around the time of the interim and final results, when there are some corporate moves, or when there is a press tip. The last two are often related, and the market may be manipulated in the case of illiquid stocks. Market makers are not beyond this either; if market makers are short of stock and need to buy some in to settle their books, sharply lowering the price quoted on screen will often shake out a panic seller.

What are the implications of this for the new issue market? The first is that if there is a danger that the stock will be very closely held and have a small free float, the price will swing between being very volatile and being completely unchanged from one day to the next. As interest dies down in the wake of the flotation and stock passes from short-term to long-term holders, volume always declines also. In these cases spreads widen and dealing sizes (Normal Market Size (NMS), in the terms of the Stock Exchange) can become very small.

It is not unknown for smaller stocks priced in tens of pence to be quoted in an NMS of one or two thousand shares, with a 10 per cent spread. In these cases dealing costs can amount to over 20 per cent of the transaction, wiping out any profits since flotation. A large holding in the stock could take some time to find a buyer, or might only be placed at an unappealing price. In these cases investors can be stuck in the stock for some time, waiting for a pick-up in dealing interest or an event to get out. So receiving a substantial allocation of stock in some new issues might generate large initial paper profits but at the expense of longer-term headaches. Investors are advised to watch out for stocks which could become very tightly held after flotation. Generally any smaller stock with a free float of less than 10 per cent of its market capitalization could be susceptible.

WHO IS THE BROKER?

Placing power is concentrated with just a handful of broking firms in the UK, as in other markets, and only a few of the integrated securities houses are capable of getting the larger issues away. An addition to this is the firm of Cazenove, already broker to more companies than any other by a factor of nearly two and able to place stock with institutions in a way no other firm can.

The consequence of this is that many broking firms in the UK have very little placing power, so may not be able to attract enough interest in some issues. Firms which are outside the top dozen or so do relatively little institutional business and therefore cannot take on the larger issues at all. However, it is also the case that some of these smaller firms specialize in certain

> **Name of the broker . . . can indicate the level of interest the firm is capable of generating.**

areas, care more about the issue in question and can build up considerable expertise. Some do not have a good reputation for acting in the long-term interests of their customers, however.

Therefore the name of the broker involved is of importance as it can indicate the level of interest the firm is capable of generating, and also perhaps bring some investors on board because of who they are. But does this mean that investors can simply rely on the reputation of the bigger firms when investing? Recent evidence shows that they cannot; some of the biggest flops have been associated with the most blue-chip names. Rothschild brought Aerostructures Hamble to the market, after all.

CHECKLIST

i   *Are the management or institutions selling out?*

ii   *Does the company rely heavily on one product, supplier or customer?*

iii   *Has the price been reduced during the marketing campaign or at the last minute? This can be a good or a bad sign – look for objective value comparisons at the new price.*

iv   *If it is a demerger, has it been saddled with too much debt?*

v   *Does the company have a controlling shareholder?*

vi   *Where is the money going?*

vii   *Is there a risk warning (usually for high technology stocks)?*

viii *If it is not already doing so, when is the company going to make a profit?*

ix   *If it is an MBO or turnaround, does the improvement seem to have come just a little too quickly?*

x   *Is there any outstanding litigation?*

xi   *Are there any regulatory or political concerns?*

xii   *Is it being hyped? Are there too many sponsors associated with the issue?*

xiii *Will there be a sufficiently liquid aftermarket? The broking firm involved can be of importance here.*

'Some of the greatest rewards and some of the greatest failures.'

5

'BLUE SKY' ISSUES

- 'Blue sky'
- Scientific research stocks
- Different listing rules apply
- Other high technology issues
- Risks and rewards
- Patent busting
- Volatility and portfolios

WHAT IS A 'BLUE SKY' ISSUE?

Some of the greatest rewards from new issues, and some of the greatest failures, have come from so-called 'blue sky' issues. These stocks are generally high technology or pharmaceutical related stocks which offer investors a chance to invest in a product at a much earlier stage of development than would otherwise be the case. They almost never pay a dividend at the time of flotation, nor do they intend to in the foreseeable future, needing to reinvest any revenue in product development.

> The hope is that the winners will soar away into the blue sky, taking investors with them.

More importantly, few of them are profitable and may not be so for many years. These stocks therefore defy conventional investment analysis, and their valuation depends solely on the 'hope factor'. The hope is that the winners will soar away into the blue sky, taking investors with them.

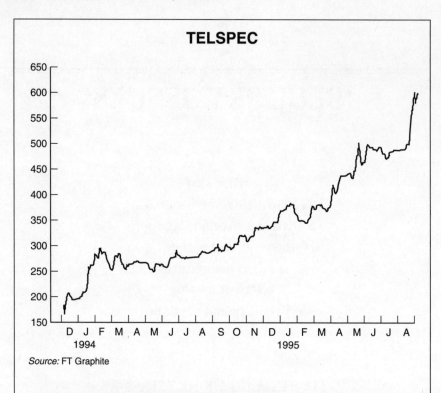

TELSPEC

Source: FT Graphite

Telspec was the best performing new issue on the UK market in 1993-94, floated at 160 pence in December 1993 and reaching a high of 384 pence just over a year later.

The story which attracted investors was of a smaller company in a vast and growing industry – telecoms equipment, with both geographical diversity (50 per cent of sales outside the UK) and sales to well-known industry leaders (British Telecom, Deutsche Telekom).

In the case of Telspec the hope factor was tempered with the reassurance that the industry was not so leading edge that its prospects were uncertain, and the fact that the group was already profitable.

The hope factor can sustain some pretty optimistic valuations for a stock, but only so long as the dream continues. For many of these stocks the bubble can burst as their products become obsolete due to competition, do not perform as well as expected, or simply do not work at all. In these cases the sentiment which supported the share price quickly evaporates and share prices can come down to earth sharply. It comes as no surprise that many of these stocks disappoint investors just at the point when the company reaches profitability and the cold reality does not justify much of the hype. This point, however, comes well after flotation.

SCIENTIFIC RESEARCH STOCKS

The last few years have seen a proliferation of biotechnology and pharmaceuticals related companies coming to the UK stock market after the Stock Exchange changed its listing rules to accommodate such companies. This was in response to the experience of the US market which was generally favourable, and demonstrated the desire of the UK authorities to be seen to be raising capital for high technology projects, of which the market was in general unfamiliar.

The flood of smaller companies which came to the market saw some spectacular performers and also some which failed to meet their investors' expectations. It should be borne in mind that these companies are almost by definition high risk as the reason for the Stock Exchange dispensation was to allow products to be financed at an earlier stage of their development than would otherwise have been the case.

Most companies coming to the stock market are required to demonstrate a three year trading record, and a record of consistent losses with the prospect of several more would not endear them to the authorities. But this is exactly the case with drug development in particular. Development of a drug to the stage where it can even be submitted for stage 1 trial can take years and several millions of pounds. Nursing the drug through stage 2 and 3 trials on to approval by each of the authorities individually in all of the major world pharmaceutical markets (basically the Western world plus Japan) can take even longer. And approval by one authority does not automatically mean a rubber stamp by others. Glaxo's Zantac, the world's best selling drug, is now approved for over-the-counter (OTC) sale in most of Europe but was refused approval by the FDA in the US.

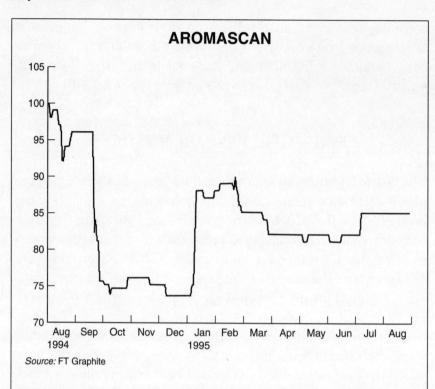

AROMASCAN

Source: FT Graphite

Aromascan had a hugely interesting product – an electronic nose with a potentially enormous number of uses, including the monitoring of foods, but strangely failed to excite investors. Just a few weeks after flotation the shares were trading at nearly 20 per cent below their issue price.

While the company had a strong product, investors were concerned that larger competitors might catch up quickly and also that the company had only enough cash for several months trading, by which time joint ventures with larger partners would need to have been signed up.

The risk is not restricted to regulatory issues only. A recent drug development issue in the UK, Cantab Pharmaceuticals, had to announce to the market well after its flotation that one of the drugs in its development portfolio had been found in stage I trials to be no better than the placebo.

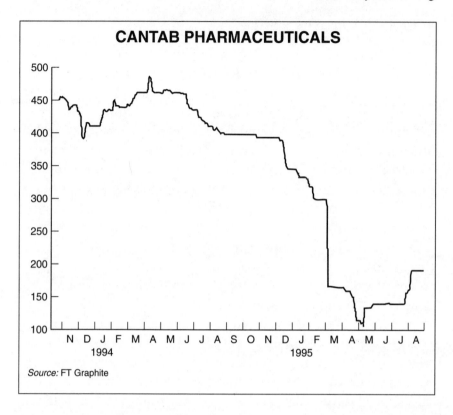

For the world's major drugs companies with their research and development expenditure measured annually in the hundreds of millions, this would be a setback, but they each have many drugs at various stages of development. Over a hundred projects can be started to produce just one commercial drug. For a smaller drug issue with only two products under development, as permitted by the Stock Exchange rules, this could be catastrophic.

The Stock Exchange definition of these companies is 'Scientific Research Based'. For them to achieve a listing a number of the standard rules are waived. They have to convince the Stock Exchange that they fall within the definition of companies which are primarily involved in the laboratory research and development of chemical or biological products or processes, including pharmaceutical companies and those involved in the areas of diagnostics, agriculture and food.

What do they need for a listing?

To obtain a full listing these companies are exempt from the requirement to have had an independent revenue earning business for three years, with accounts to match. They are also exempt from a number of other new issue requirements, including those which determine how shares should be marketed in a new issue. The Stock Exchange's Listing Rules require an offer for sale element in issues of over £25m. The relaxation of these rules follows the successful example of the US NASDAQ market, which has attracted a large number of popular high-tech issues.

However, they do have to comply with another set of requirements specific to the sector. The three year rule is modified in that the company must demonstrate that it has at least a three year record of operations in laboratory research and development and that it has the ability to attract funds from sophisticated investors. It must also have achieved significant commercial milestones.

These are valuable safeguards for the less sophisticated investor, which includes even professional fund managers when dealing with these products. Making sure the product has reached a certain stage of development whereby others in the same industry are prepared to take an interest protects subsequent investors to some extent, but it does not prevent drugs not working as well as expected, costing too much or being superseded.

Significant commercial milestones are considered to be the expenditure of more than £20m over a period of three years or more which has created intellectual property, or a current development agreement with another independent company where the other party has committed at least £5m.

Another way of satisfying this requirement is to have at least two drugs in clinical trial under internationally accepted regulatory scrutiny. This demonstrates succinctly the risks of drugs companies. If one of these does not work in the end the company could be in trouble, or at the very least a lot of investors' money will have been wasted. That said, relying on two drugs which have passed trials and been approved in a number of countries is not a cause for great concern. Many of the world's pharmaceutical leaders, including the now merged Glaxo and Wellcome, make the bulk of their revenue from less than a dozen blockbuster drugs.

How much has to be raised?

Bringing a scientific research based company to a full listing requires it to be raising at least £10m and have a capitalization at the issue price of at least £20m, excluding shares issued within the last six months. In the field of scientific development, £10m does not go far and investors should be prepared for consistent equity raising to further develop the products, nurse them through trials and ultimately market them.

In the case of a winner this is no bad thing as shareholders in the UK retain their pre-emption rights and have first refusal on further substantial equity raising. However, Glaxo has now gone for a genera-tion without a rights issue so this is not always the case.

> **Investors should be prepared for consistent equity raising to further develop the products.**

In practice few drugs, except those of the giants, now get to the market solely through the efforts of just one company, and joint ventures are the order of the day. The presence of a larger partner, often with an equity stake in the business either prior to or as a part of the process of bringing the company to the market, is a reassurance to less sophisticated investors. They can be sure that an industry professional thinks the project worth a go and that lack of funding for development is less likely to be a concern.

Locking in of major shareholders

These major shareholders, as well as directors, are locked into the company more so than is the case in conventional new issues. Without the permission of the authorities, major shareholders (with more than a 3 per cent stake or the right to nominate direc-tors) at the time of the listing may not dispose of any shares within six months, or within six months after the next set of results after dealings commence.

These shareholders are further required to hold 40 per cent of their stake for a period of two years. While this serves to lock the original backers of the company in, it can of course lead to the company having shareholders who want out, and an overhang of shares likely to come on to the market as soon as possible which would depress prices. Directors and former directors of these companies are locked in for two years, the restriction applying to their entire holdings.

The listing particulars

In addition to the normal information required of a set of listing particulars, a scientific research based company must detail any patents granted or applications in progress and provide an estimate of funding resources for the next two years. The estimate must be accompanied by an assurance that the funds can be met out of existing resources and those to be raised.

This is to ensure that the company does not come back to shareholders for more money shortly after the issue. The company should demonstrate in most cases that it has engaged in research with other organizations in the industry and give details on the products themselves. These should include information on research, development status, risks, competitors, future strategies and, crucially, revenue generation. Specifically, the company should disclose whether it intends to go it alone with the product development or in collaboration with others in the industry. Details of any copyrights associated with software should also be present.

Patent busting

A relatively recent development in the pharmaceuticals industry has been that of patent busting. Provided that a patent has been validly applied for and granted, a manufacturer has exclusive rights to production and marketing of the drug for a period of several years.

Thereafter the patent expires and while the original producer may still retain the rights to the brand name, other 'generic' drugs manufacturers can produce and market their own versions of the drug. As certain blockbuster drugs can be hugely profitable, there is money to be made from disputing the validity or ownership of a patent.

It has now become commonplace in the US (of course one of the world's biggest drugs markets) for patent busting applications to be made either to dispute the validity, or the rightful ownership, of a patent. The same applies to other intellectual property such as copyright.

Often the intention of the suit is to allow generic drugs manufacturers to produce their versions of the drug immediately without waiting for patent expiry. This practice of course strikes at the very basis of the patent system, which is designed to allow developers of a product to recoup their costs and profit before others can come on the scene to use their research, having made no prior investment.

Nevertheless, patent busting is big business and few large pharmaceutical companies are not now engaged in legal action on a virtually permanent basis. The advent of patent busting cases for a smaller company should not be underestimated as the costs of

Patent busting is big business.

fighting a case can be substantial. More importantly share prices can be depressed as investors can be concerned that the assets in which they are supposedly investing could be handed over to somebody else by the courts.

Problems are exacerbated by the long time taken to resolve these cases in court, sometimes the better part of a decade. In some cases the value of the patent comes to dwarf the assets of the company involved. Although not a scientific development company as such, the shares in Rodime have traded more on the hopes for settlement of its case over a computer diskette than on its trading performance. The size of awards in a legal case can be such that, as in the case of Rodime, the potential award can be many times the value of the company.

Based on the market maxim that you should invest only in something that is well understood, it might be best to leave court disputes to lawyers and avoid pharmaceuticals companies involved in protracted litigation.

The life of a drug product

The nature of some illnesses is that the drugs needed to combat them will always require skilled medical staff to administer. These drugs can be hugely expensive and therefore make large amounts of money for the companies which developed them, but they will always have a relatively limited application and remain 'prescription only' in most developed medical systems. When their patents expire, or they are superseded beforehand by better drugs from other manufacturers, the medical profession will move on to other drugs unless their relative prices influence the decision as to what drug is administered to patients (see below).

These products do not in general acquire brand names known to the public at large. Most patients take what is prescribed to them by their doctor, although it is the case that in the US AIDS patients have become very vocal in lobbying for certain drugs to be administered and adopted by the medical profession. For a drug which will always remain a prescription product due to the nature of the condition it is treating or its inherent risks and side effects, there is relatively little growth prospect after its patent expiry. Generic drugs manufacturers will step in and with few development costs to cover sell the same drug formulation to physicians and health services at a lower cost. While the original manufacturer can count on some brand name recognition from doctors, prices inevitably fall. However, it has recently been demonstrated that the decline in sales of a brand leader when generic competition is introduced is less dramatic than had been predicted.

For other drugs the situation is different. If the drug, even in a reduced dosage format, can be marketed safely to the general public in Over The Counter (OTC) form, the drug can be treated more as a conventional product and less like a drug. The manufacturer will always seek where possible to maintain higher prices and margins while the drug has the protection of a patent, but thereafter there is huge potential as an OTC product.

While there may be competition, consumers buy the brand names they recognize, and brand names are now valued somewhat controversially in the balance sheets of a number of large companies.

The advantage of the OTC market is that it extends the life cycle of a drug. While the medical establishment will usually prescribe either the most effective or the most cost-effective treatment, the general public has a long history of buying medicines which they do not need or which are of doubtful effectiveness on the basis of brand recognition.

Prescription drugs which receive OTC approval have the advantage that patients who took the drug when it was prescribed by their doctor will later buy the product in OTC form. The great advantage for the manufacturer is that brand names are intangible and can lead to very high margins. It is perfectly possible in the UK to buy paracetamol tablets in large bottles for next to nothing, but as a result of television and other advertising the public prefers to buy slick packaging and brand names it recognizes. The effectiveness of the drug in relieving headaches is identical.

So what does this mean for pharmaceutical companies? It means that not all drugs have the same prospects and those which are likely to achieve brand name status in the aftermarket will probably have a longer life, and hence possibly higher valuation in the market, than specialist drugs. There is huge pressure from overstretched health services to restrict the number of drugs prescribed and encourage more treatment through OTC drugs, so the likelihood is that any drug which treats a common complaint will receive OTC approval in the long run. This is in addition to the self-evident point that drugs to treat a condition suffered by a large proportion of the public are likely to generate a larger income stream over the years than those for obscure diseases.

The recent practice of the pharmaceuticals industry has been to farm out drugs towards the end of their life cycles to specialists in the manufacture and marketing of generic drugs in joint ventures, or for specialist drugs companies to bring in a partner with better distribution and marketing for an OTC product. The most successful of these in stock market terms has been Medeva, which now has a portfolio of generic drugs which it markets in a large number of countries. These companies do still have research and development needs in order to satisfy regulatory authorities, and it could well be the case that the next few years see a number of

specialist drugs companies coming to the market for funds to support the marketing of drugs towards the end of their life cycles
rather than those in the earliest stages of development.

Not all these companies make drugs

It is not always the case that the medical establishment agrees
wholeheartedly that a drug actually works. Regina struggled on for
many years on the stock market on the basis of a single product,
that of royal jelly, as made by bees. Many people swear by the
product and the company no doubt has numerous studies to show
its beneficial effects. Nevertheless, the stock market never believed
that royal jelly did anybody any more good than the other primary
product of the bee, honey. Brokers, analysts and investors are uni-
formly cynical, and experience of the market over the years has
taught them to be.

The point to be made is that if there is a degree of doubt about
the efficacy of a product, the astronomical ratings accorded to

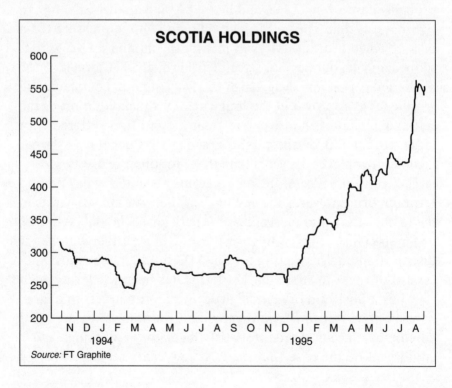

some true pharmaceutical stocks will not be attainable. A relatively recent new issue, Scotia, struggled at below its issue price for some time, having had its debut pulled once, because of market scepticism that its primary product, oil of evening primrose, had any medical value. It was only when Scotia persuaded the market that it was developing 'true' drug products as a treatment for conditions such as cancer and diabetes-induced blindness that its share price took off.

Drugs are not a licence to print money

While the pharmaceuticals industry undoubtedly operates with much better margins than most manufacturing companies, legal drugs are not a licence to print money. The margins of the drugs companies are artificially sustained by the patent system and the tacit admission by regulatory authorities that enough money has to be made from the sale of successful drugs to pay for those which never proved their worth and for the development of the next generation.

However, both the national health services of Europe and private medical insurance schemes are now under pressure from the soaring costs of drugs and are unable to pay for all the treatments on the market. Drug prices are subject to control in many European countries, and in the US the health providers have moved into alliances with distributors large enough to be able to put pressure on the drug manufacturers to reduce prices.

It is therefore the case that the developer of any future blockbuster drug might not see quite the enthusiastic demand for its product as has been the case in the past. There is considerable resistance, for example, to the extension of Wellcome's AIDS treatment to HIV-positive patients who have not yet developed AIDS, motivated in part by considerations of cost.

The leading pharmaceutical companies in the FT-SE 100 may be more mature stocks without the explosive growth of some of the small companies coming to the market, but in the past they traded at substantial p/e premiums. Now they even yield more than the market average in some cases.

HIGH TECHNOLOGY APPLICATIONS

The caveats which apply to drugs companies apply equally to high technology companies. Many of these companies depend for most of their revenue (and hope factor) on just one product, which brings with it all of the problems referred to in Chapter 4.

But what investors have to fear in addition to these factors is the danger of obsolescence before the product has generated enough revenue to repay its investment. This is less likely with drug stocks because of their longer development times and relatively water-tight patents, but high technology applications frequently have very brief lives before being superseded. Witness the growth in power of personal computers and the rapid obsolescence of older processing chips. The technology is also less comprehensively proven than is the case with pharmaceutical applications, and may simply not work in the end.

> **Many of these companies depend for most of their revenue . . . on just one product.**

However, these stocks also offer the opportunity to be in at the ground floor with a world beating product – a new Microsoft.

Volatility

Because high technology stocks depend for so much of their performance on the hope factor, their day-to-day performance on the stock market can be very volatile in price terms. Sentiment can change very quickly if another similar product appears on the horizon, and these changes are exacerbated by relatively illiquid markets, producing rapid price falls. On the other hand, any good news will prompt an immediate stock shortage, driving the price much higher than might otherwise be justified.

Higher than normal volatility is also seen in the overall performance of the companies in the sector. For more conventional companies with a broad range of products, customers and suppliers, any upturn or downturn in business is more gradual and less spectacular. With high technology companies, they either succeed

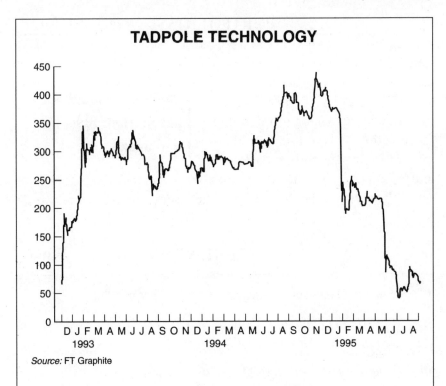

TADPOLE TECHNOLOGY

Source: FT Graphite

Tadpole Technology was for some considerable time one of the darlings of the high technology sector, having developed an advanced
notebook computer called the Sparcbook. Tadpole shares performed
well for some months, albeit subject to some volatility, but dropped
abruptly when it became evident that there had been some production delays. A second profits warning just a few weeks later saw the
shares plunge to half their placing price. The new management team
appointed an adviser to assist in a possible sale of the business to a
larger partner.

Tadpole also became well known for being one of those stocks
where the price always fell before negative information was released
to the stock market, another potential pitfall of smaller companies.

brilliantly or disappear ignominiously. In the last two years both
the best and the worst performing new issues came from the high
technology sector, and the range of performance was much greater
than for the market as a whole.

PORTFOLIOS

The lesson for investors in 'blue sky' issues is that a portfolio investment approach is needed more than ever. There are no certain winners or losers in this sector, more so than in any other, so investors should not put all their eggs in one basket. A portfolio is required, in which 'over time' the winners should outweigh the losers.

Investors should not put all their eggs in one basket.

CHECKLIST

i   *How much are you paying for the hope factor?*

ii *When is the company likely to make a profit, or at least break even at the operational level?*

iii *Is there a risk warning? (There usually is.)*

iv *How many products has the company got? How close are they to the market?*

v   *Are there any major partners?*

vi *Is there a risk of patent busting actions, or have they already started? Are there any legal disputes?*

vii *How long are major shareholders locked in?*

viii *Beware the volatility of these stocks; always maintain a portfolio.*

'These projects live or die on the forecasts they make at the time they come to the market.'

6

MAJOR CAPITAL PROJECTS

- **Eurotunnel and Euro Disney**
- **Cable television**
- **What's wrong with major capital projects?**
- **Forecasts and revenues**
- **Volatility**

'BETTER TO TRAVEL HOPEFULLY THAN ARRIVE'

The investment management industry in the UK is constantly being berated by industrialists for its short-termism in looking for performance over months rather than years. It is these same industrialists who sit as trustees for these same funds and regularly switch managers for underperformance. That said, the typical UK investor wants performance now and is unimpressed by 'jam tomorrow' arguments.

In this context the UK market is highly sceptical of huge capital intensive projects, and the limited experience to date has shown this to be perfectly justified. Both Euro Disney and Eurotunnel, the two largest projects of the sort to date in the UK, have at times proved disastrous for investors.

Both of these issues have been listed on the Paris Bourse as well as the UK Stock Exchange and the French market has often been seen to support the share price when UK investors have been heavy sellers. Indeed, by the time Eurotunnel started carrying passengers three-quarters of the issue, originally marketed equally in France and the UK, was in French hands.

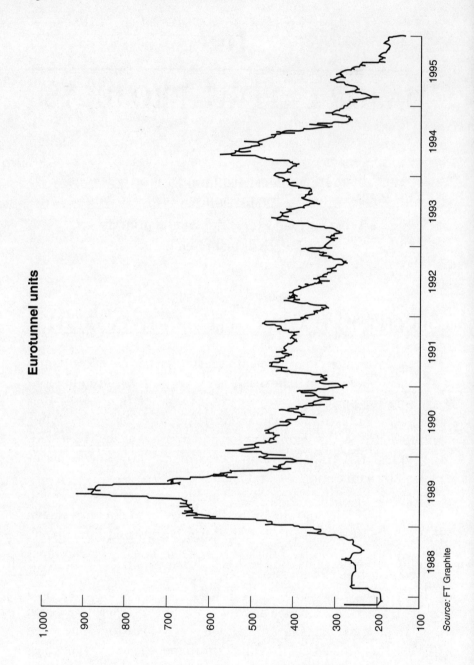

Eurotunnel units

Source: FT Graphite

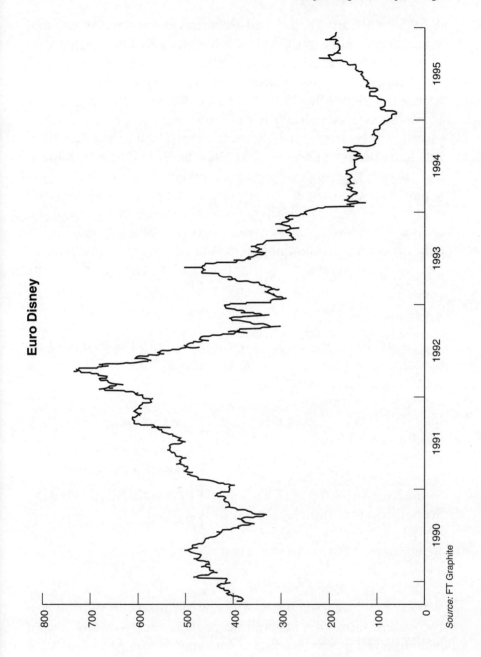

Euro Disney

Source: FT Graphite

Although Euro Disney and Eurotunnel underperformed the market very badly in the years following their (very well publicized) flotations, their initial performance was very strong. Some significant profits were realized in the early days and months following flotation. Euro Disney, for instance, was floated at a price of FF 72, reached an (adjusted) all-time high of FF 165, but had to be supported by a cash injection from Saudi prince Alwaleed Bin Talal Bin Abdulaziz in 1994 after the Walt Disney Company walked away from supporting any more rights issues.

Similarly, Eurotunnel was floated at 290 pence in 1987, reached a high of 350 pence well before trading commenced, and dropped to its all time low of 140 pence, as fears of a debt rescheduling or debt for equity swop mounted, in August 1995 – several months after Le Shuttle and the Eurostar train had started running.

Travelling hopefully

The lesson for the new issues investor in the Euro Disney and Eurotunnel issues is that these stocks disappointed the market most when they actually started trading. Up to that point any investment decision was a value judgement on the credibility of the forecasts on which the whole edifice was built. If the consensus of the market was in favour of belief the share price performed very well for long periods. Sceptics were ultimately proved right time and again as forecasts were missed, but only the most sophisticated of investors are able to maintain a short position in a stock for a very long period.

> **These stocks disappointed the market most when they actually started trading.**

What eventually happened was that the market polarized into two camps: those who believed the projects were going to succeed without revising their forecasts and moving the goalposts, and those who would never touch the stocks. Euro Disney now looks to be on course to make money in 1996, seven years after building started, and at that point will attract a whole new investor base. Those who stuck with it through the lean years have not been rewarded.

Similarly, Eurotunnel could well pay a dividend in 2003 as it is now forecasting, but previous forecasts were woefully inaccurate. Stock market wags at the time commented that it would be better to invest in the revenue forecasts of the Eurotunnel brokers, which were constantly rising, than in the share price, which was not.

WHAT IS A MAJOR CAPITAL PROJECT?

The Stock Exchange defines issues such as Eurotunnel as 'Companies Undertaking Major Capital Projects' and will allow such companies to list their shares even if they cannot comply with the standard rules which require audited accounts for three years and a history of revenue generating business activities.

The project must have no obvious access to other funding sources, perhaps indicating a degree of unwillingness on the part of the Stock Exchange to encourage such issues. The minimum to be raised in the issue must be £50m and the total capital requirement at least £100m. The listing particulars are required to show detailed cash flow, profit and dividend projections for the next three years or longer if relevant. However, unlike other special case issues, there is no requirement for the issuer to prove that there will be no recourse to the market for further funds within a specified period.

More major capital projects could well be seen coming to the UK market in the near future as a consequence of the Tory government's Private Finance Initiative to fund infrastructure projects with private rather than public capital. Whether this will survive any change of administration remains to be seen. While the Eurotunnel issue might make investors justifiably cautious of committing their money to such schemes, the experience of such projects has not been all bad. The Dartford bridge, built many years after the Dartford tunnel, was built largely on schedule and within budget, and has a secure revenue base to repay any investment. Similar schemes could work very well.

WHAT IS THE PROBLEM WITH THESE PROJECTS?

The problem with all of these projects in essence is that they can easily starve through lack of funds, and they live and die on the forecasts they make at the time they come to the market. Bear in mind that most of the highly paid analysts in the City will not forecast the profits of the companies they cover more than two years ahead – the current year, where they have usually had a steer from the finance director as to how things are going, and next year. Even then there are often disappointments and surprises.

A major capital project makes forecasts for both revenues and costs for up to 20 years ahead. Most of the forecasts made this far ahead could reasonably be considered to be a fantasy created in the mind of the company's own analysts. They may be based on the most conservative estimates, but nobody can forecast that far ahead with any degree of accuracy.

The second problem for such projects is that they have no safety cushion. When a company embarks on a new venture or product launch, it generally has the resources from its other current trading operations to cope with cost overruns and delays (beware the ones which do not). With a major project where there is no revenue coming in, any cost overruns and delays have to be financed by further recourse to either the banks (who are receiving no interest income or repayments, of course) or to shareholders (who are seeing no returns). Both Eurotunnel and Euro Disney have come to shareholders several times for money, and were put off from doing so only when a fall in the share price made further equity issues inadvisable. Both came to the stage where they were holding the banks hostage for further funds, threatening the loss of money so far committed.

Investors should look hard at when the project is going to generate some revenue.

WHEN IS SOME REVENUE GOING TO COME IN?

Given the problems associated with forecasting both costs and revenues several years ahead, it is fair to say that as costs can be calculated more accurately than revenues because there are fewer external factors, investors should look hard at when the project is going to generate some revenue. These projects create a huge asset when completed, but this is of no value to equity investors if the project has been put into liquidation just when it is completed because there is still no revenue to repay the banks.

A project which is going to generate revenue in three years' time, even if not enough to cover interest costs, is inherently less risky than one which is going to see its first customer in ten years' time. On the other hand, the volatility of revenue forecasts could lead to a situation in which forecasts are seen to be too conservative and the project lays the golden egg. Experience has shown it would be wise to be sceptical, however.

VOLATILITY AND VALUATIONS

As no revenue is being generated by these issues, conventional valuation methods for share issues such as price/earnings ratios and yields cannot be applied. The most common valuation of these issues is the discounted cash flow calculation, based on the estimated dividend income from the stock when it starts paying dividends.

The value of the dividend stream over the next 20 years (beyond that has little effect on the calculation) is discounted at a given interest rate to arrive at a net present value of the income stream, which should give some indication of the value of the stock to a pension fund investor who invests for yield.

Stock price is more than ever subject to the vagaries of sentiment.

The problem with discounted cash flow calculations is that they are very sensitive to the interest rate assumptions made in the calculation, and results can differ widely as a result of relatively small adjustments in the assumptions made. This is merely a further illustration of the problems of forecasting several years ahead. The consequence of the difficulty in valuing these stocks on any sort of objective basis is that stock price is more than ever subject to the vagaries of sentiment. This can mean a much more volatile share price, with prices going down as well as up. When sentiment changes towards the market as a whole, issues of this nature can suffer disproportionately as professional investors demonstrate a 'flight to safety', i.e. to conservatively valued, higher yielding stocks.

THE NEXT GENERATION

The next generation of major capital projects is cable television and telecommunications. The experience of the satellite television industry in the UK is mixed. Sky looked the better bet after BSB took too long to get off the ground, but after the merger of the two operations has gone from strength to strength. Cable operators do at least have a partially exclusive franchise in their areas, in as much as nobody else is allowed to dig the road up and install an infrastructure. It may well be, however, that competitors do not need to. Cable television firms are potentially in trouble on their revenue forecasts if British Telecom ever gets the go-ahead for video on demand.

The analogy between cable television and its predecessors, Euro Disney and Eurotunnel, is obvious. All of these spend a large sum of money building (and digging) to create a huge asset, which the general public is then invited to use. The ultimate value of the asset, which cannot be used for any other purpose, depends on the willingness of the public to use it. This is a crucial difference between these major projects and most other companies. At least a proportion of the assets of most trading or investment companies can be used for some other purpose, giving the company a break-up value in the last resort. The assets of a major project cannot be moved and cannot be used for anything else – a point highlighted by Eurotunnel itself, when it positioned a huge tunnel boring machine with a 'For Sale' sign on it as an advertisement by the side of the road leading to the terminal.

The cable television companies have to have access to large sums of money to dig up every street in their franchise area in order to install the cabling necessary to deliver the service. At 1995 estimates it cost £25 to £35 for each metre of cable installed. Now the cost of cabling an entire area can be estimated quite accurately, not least because it is a relatively low-tech operation capable of being done manually with spades. The cost of the technology is also easily estimated, although upgrades to cope with more sophisticated competition are a possibility.

For these companies everything depends on the willingness of the general public to subscribe to the television and telephone (most have chosen to lead with telecoms) services they offer. More importantly, they depend on the take-up of higher margin, added value services. Existing television and telephone services are inherently cheaper to deliver than cable services, not least because digging the road up is expensive, and while British Telecom dug roads up, it did so years ago and has long since written off the cost. The basic calculation that can be applied to cable telecoms is that of payback time: how many subscribers does it need, and for how long, to pay back the costs of delivering the service to them in the first place.

Why have cable television issues underperformed?

The UK investment community is, needless to say, sceptical of cable television. The first of the issues to attempt a market listing, TeleWest, had the issue pulled first time around due to 'market conditions' (i.e. lack of interest at the price hoped for). It later did make a successful market debut, albeit with the help of several battalions of brokers pushing the issue to the institutions. Later performance has been mediocre and is set to suffer from the problems of its successors.

The later General Cable issue first indicated a price in the range 225 to 260 pence when its marketing campaign commenced, but later had to scale the issue back dramatically to 190 pence to get it away after a lack of investor interest. The price still went to a discount on the first day of trading, as happened with Nynex CableComms to a lesser extent but after a late surge of interest.

Only a proportion of the investment community believes in cable telecoms, and the funds controlled by these people may be switched out of TeleWest, the first issue, into subsequent issues such as General Cable. It could well prove to be the case that the sector constantly sees the funds shifting into the newer issues, or vice versa as the companies mature and come closer to generating sufficient revenue.

One reason for market scepticism of cable television is perhaps a cultural one. Proportionately fewer City folk use satellite or cable television than in the population as a whole. It is regarded as a C2 product in terms of demographics, rather than being used by the AB/C1 groupings into which most of the City falls. One axiom of investing is that you should only invest in what you understand. The City may well turn out to be wrong, but Chancellor Nigel Lawson criticized the 'teenage scribblers' (young financial analysts) in the City in the 1980s to his cost. They were right in the end.

CHECKLIST

i   *How long is it before any revenue comes in?*

ii   *How long is it before a profit is forecast?*

iii   *When will dividends commence?*

iv   *Does the project have any major backers? Are they locked in?*

v   *How much contingency reserve is there in the capital requirements?*

vi   *Are there any new technological risks?*

vii   *Are any competitor projects on the horizon?*

viii   *Are there any calculations for the Net Present Value of the dividend stream?*

ix   *Beware the volatility of share prices.*

x   *It may be better to travel hopefully than arrive with some of these!*

'Mineral companies operate in unique circumstances.'

7

MINERAL, OIL AND GAS COMPANIES

- **Special rules apply for listings**
- **Effect of commodity prices**
- **Share prices volatile**
- **Asset plays**
- **Political risk**

FEW ISSUES THESE DAYS

Very few oil and gas or mining companies have come to the market in recent years in the world's developed stock markets. In part, this is because the major players in the industry are already quoted and there has been a trend towards consolidation by takeover, but in the case of smaller stocks it is also because the market has good cause to treat such issues with caution.

New issues by flotation are unlikely in the Exploration and Production (E&P) sector because there are still a number of casualties of the last stream of these issues in the 1980s which exist as shell companies and which could be used as vehicles for reverse takeovers.

Investors are wary of smaller mineral oil and gas companies because those with longer memories can remember rapid share price rises followed by a string of disappointments. There are very few experienced stock market players who have not lost their shirt on at least one of these stocks.

SPECIAL RULES

The UK Stock Exchange has special rules for the listing of minerals, oil and gas companies to take account of the nature of such projects. They have to be involved in mineral extraction, which includes the working of mine tailings or waste dumps in addition to more conventional projects. Companies involved only in the exploration of mineral resources which are not proposing to undertake extraction are not permitted a listing, although in the case of some oil E&P stocks this definition seems to have become a little blurred.

COMMODITY PRICES

The vast majority of smaller oil, gas and other natural resources companies quoted on the stock markets of the world are regarded by investors as commodity plays. That is, the value of the company fluctuates with the value of the natural resources it extracts from the ground. This is a simplistic but not wholly unreasonable rule of thumb, as the costs of extraction and distribution generally remain relatively fixed. Commodities are traded on an international basis in the futures markets with only minor local pricing irregularities, so it is easy, once investors know the fixed costs of the business, to work out the likely levels of profitability for a given commodity price.

Most new mining and oil and gas developments in the world today take place in areas of marginal value.

The problem for the company arises when the market price of what it produces falls below the cost of extraction. It is a reasonable assumption that most new mining and oil and gas developments in the world today take place in areas of marginal value. All the easy sources of supply were developed years ago and are in the hands of established producers.

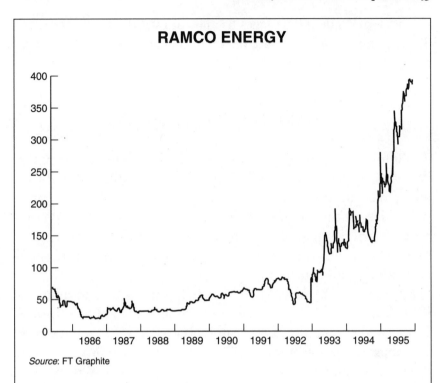

RAMCO ENERGY

Source: FT Graphite

The upside of smaller E&P stocks allying with larger partners is demonstrated by the experience of Ramco, which got into bed with a number of the world's oil majors in developing oil fields in the former Soviet state of Azerbaijan. While the price was subject to some volatility as the Russian and Azerbaijan governments argued over ownership of the oil, Ramco stood to benefit significantly even though its direct interest in the deal was only a few per cent of the total.

An exception to this may be the oil, gas and commodity fields of the former Soviet Union where a history of under-investment has created many opportunities to lend modern equipment and techniques.

These apart, most new developments come in areas where only modern technology has made it possible to extract the minerals (such as deep sea oil fields). The viability of these developments as commercial projects varies in direct proportion to the value of the mineral on the world market. There are numerous known but untapped oil fields in the world which will only become viable if the price of crude oil manages to make it over the $20/barrel level. There is no point extracting oil when it costs $20 a barrel to produce and can only be sold for $17.

SHARE PRICE VOLATILITY

The implications of this for new companies coming to the market is that the value of their shares is likely to be volatile and to fluctuate in line with the value of the underlying commodity. They are a derivative on the value of the underlying commodity, and commodity prices themselves can be very volatile on the futures markets. Not only industrial users participate in the futures markets, but also investment funds.

Investors in any new oil and gas play should bear in mind the likely volatility of share prices and the influence of asset prices. Profits and earnings forecasts can look very healthy on current oil or copper prices but look shaky if economic or political factors depress prices. Conversely, asset values can also soar at short notice, usually due to the reaction of the futures markets to some political event.

FINANCE

Tiny oil exploration and production companies have been a graveyard for investors' money over the years and have as a result produced a large number of 'shell' vehicles. The reason for this is that smaller E&P stocks rarely have many assets; in fact their only asset often comprises a small percentage interest in one or several oil or gas fields. Developing these fields usually takes vast amounts of money and is done by the oil majors with the minnows taking a cut based on their stake.

Lack of sufficient finance has been endemic to the oil minnows and the market became accustomed in the past to a string of rights issues to fund each new project. Until fields commence production these companies drain their cash on feasibility projects, head office costs and directors' salaries. These stocks are required to prove at the time of listing that, where they do not hold a controlling interest, they have a reasonable spread of investments and by voting rights or otherwise can have an influence over the timing and method of extraction. That said, there is no substitute for direct control. Experience has shown that in other cases, such as property investments, investors apply a discount both for their own lack of control and for any restrictions on realization of assets on the company itself.

For mineral companies to obtain a full Stock Exchange listing they are required to give details of working capital requirements for at least two years following the listing to ensure that they do not return to investors for more finance immediately. However, given that the financing assumptions of the company can easily be upset by movements in commodity prices these should perhaps be treated with a pinch of salt.

RESERVES

Many companies are traded more as an asset play – that is for the value of what they own which is still in the ground rather than on the basis of current production. This is calculated as a net asset value per share after deducting the company's debt, but is of course tempered by considerations of the cost of extraction. The value of the assets of the company depend on its proven and probable reserves.

Proven reserves for oil and gas stocks are those which, taking into account technical economic factors, have a better than 90 per cent chance of being produced, and for other mineral companies those which studies and measurement have indicated can be extracted under specified economic conditions.

The value of the assets of the company depend on its proven and probable reserves.

Probable reserves means those oil and gas deposits which have a better than 50 per cent chance of being produced, and for other minerals those which do not qualify as proven but whose extraction can be justified in some circumstances. In the prospectus, the term 'measured mineral resource' carries greater certainty than 'indicated mineral resource'.

Companies coming to the market must demonstrate that the aggregate value of their proven and probable reserves is at least half the value of the aggregate market value of the company's equity at the time of listing. They are also required to prove that there are sufficient reserves for production for two years following the listing or two years following the start of production, whichever is the later. In practice, investors would probably consider this an unreasonably short time and would look to see reserves at anticipated production levels for several more years.

OTHER RESTRICTIONS

Mineral extraction companies are exempted from the Stock Exchange requirement to show accounts and a trading history going back three years. Instead, investors must rely on the other details given in the prospectus to ascertain the viability of any project. However, they do have some protection in that the directors of any company seeking a listing in this way must agree, unless there is a dispensation from the Stock Exchange, not to dispose of any of their shares for a period of two years from the date dealings commence.

POLITICAL RISK

It is not universally true that mineral extraction projects are always undertaken in remote places where investors are subject to economic and political risks greater than with most stocks, but mineral companies do operate in unique circumstances. Mineral resources, especially oil and gas, are regarded as special by most governments, which in almost all cases control the issue of licences.

In the case of the former Soviet Union there has even been dispute between successor governments as to ownership of the assets and the right to control development of them. Because of the greater interest demonstrated in the ownership of mineral wealth, the companies developing them are subject to considerably more political risk than straight trading companies.

The era of widespread nationalization without compensation of oil companies has now probably passed, but political factors can still be relevant, not least because oil is the primary earner of foreign exchange for many countries. Countries themselves can be subjected to sanctions which can effectively prevent Western based companies from operating. And finally, there can be problems remitting earnings from some countries due to foreign exchange restrictions, although this is relatively unusual with products earning hard currency revenues.

ASHANTI GOLD

Ashanti Gold was one of few mining stocks to come to the market in recent years, and certainly one of the biggest with a valuation of $1.67bn at the $20/share issue price.

The issue was run on a global basis and, despite the lacklustre performance of gold as an investment, attracted applications for more than 100m shares compared with the 20.2m on offer.

The stock was subsequently priced at the top of the $17 to $20 range, but achieved a first day premium of just 3 per cent, when trading opened on SEAQ International in London.

Most of the shares were sold by the Ghanaian government, with UK conglomerate Lonrho retaining a 43 per cent stake.

CHECKLIST

---

i   *Are there any major partners?*

ii   *What are the proven or likely reserves? How long will they last at anticipated production rates.*

iii *At what price is it uneconomic to get the material out of the ground?*

iv   *Is there any political risk? Can earnings be freely taken out of the country?*

v   *Are any of the major shareholders locked in?*

vi   *Beware the effect of potentially volatile commodity prices on share prices.*

'A popular sector in terms of new issues.'

8

PROPERTY STOCKS

- ● **Investment and development property**
- ● **Covenant**
- ● **Net asset values**
- ● **Control**
- ● **Discount to net assets**
- ● **Yield**

THE PROPERTY MARKET

Property companies were the growth stocks of the 1980s Lawson boom in the UK when huge fortunes were made in the development property market. Two of the most famous were Stanhope and Rosehaugh, which jointly developed the Broadgate Centre over Liverpool Street Station in the City. Broadgate has now become a highly prized location and the effective centre of the City, but what happened to its developers? Rosehaugh is in the hands of the receivers, while Stanhope was bid for by British Land at just 3 pence per share after doing a deal with the banks over its debt.

Of those that have survived, many others now populate the lower reaches of the market where they may yet be used as shell vehicles for the next generation of market entrepreneurs. But property is not necessarily a poor investment, even if it has lost the golden

> **Property is not necessarily a poor investment, even if it has lost the golden egg status it used to have.**

egg status it used to have. There is now an oversupply of investment and development property in the UK, especially in London, so investment has to be a little more selective, but property remains a popular sector in terms of new issues. In 1993 and 1994 property issues accounted for 11.8 per cent of all flotations compared with its value of 2.0 per cent of the FT-All Share.

As with other sectors of the market, institutions are amongst the largest holders of property stocks. They are also large direct holders of property investments, funding many of the larger developments themselves, and are some of the largest landlords in the country. But there is some evidence that institutions, especially the smaller ones, are switching out of direct property investment in favour of holdings in property stocks, attracted by the greater portfolio diversity and liquidity of holdings.

INVESTMENT AND DEVELOPMENT PROPERTY

Development property was the darling of the 1980s, but it has always been investment property which has been the chosen institutional investment asset. Investment property is that which has an incumbent tenant paying rent, and therefore has a steady income stream, and so is valued primarily on a yield basis.

Development property is that which has no incumbent tenant, and is in theory either being built or redeveloped to increase its attractiveness to potential occupiers, and therefore its value. In times when property values are increasing rapidly due to a shortage of supply, the capital value of property held for redevelopment can increase substantially.

> **Investment property, . . . has a broader range of potential buyers as it yields a more immediate and tangible investment return.**

The problem with development property is that there is no certainty that anybody will want to occupy it, or they might need substantial incentives to occupy it. In the meantime the developer has to pay the continued costs of maintaining it. There have been

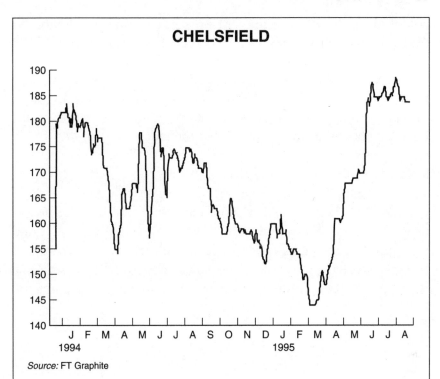

CHELSFIELD

Source: FT Graphite

The performance of Chelsfield demonstrates the importance of backing well-respected management teams. Chelsfield, run by well-known figure in the property world Elliott Bernard, existed for many years as a private company and came to the market only at the end of 1993.

Bernard retained a controlling stake, and no shares were sold by existing investors in the £50m cash raising – all of it went to the company to fund further expansion.

While the share price did little over the next 12 months, this was due primarily to uncertainty in the property market – Chelsfield outperformed the sector by 33 per cent. But this does illustrate the greater exposure to market risk inherent in property stocks.

Chelsfield is known as a developer and accordingly got away with a yield of under half the market average.

recent examples of development property companies, unable to find tenants, deliberately making their assets uninhabitable in order to avoid paying rates.

Because the value of any asset ultimately depends on the willingness of somebody else to buy it, valuations of development property have to be treated with some caution. There are always buyers to be found for property, but the market is well known for its aggressive negotiators and any developer selling under pressure from costs will not achieve a decent price.

Investment property, on the other hand, has a broader range of potential buyers as it yields a more immediate and tangible investment return. For this reason valuations are more representative and probably more reliable. Given these considerations, an investment property stock should trade at a smaller discount to net asset value than a development property stock as there is a smaller risk premium.

COVENANT

The attractiveness of investment property depends on the quality of the covenant, i.e. the quality of the tenant in the property. FTSE 100 or well-known large companies are better covenants than others, but also have substantial bargaining power when negotiating to occupy the property in the first place, so can reduce the rent they ultimately pay. In today's over-supplied property market prospective tenants can also demand rent free periods or other incentives to occupy. The bargaining position of blue chip tenants notwithstanding, they contribute significantly to the quality of covenant as they are very unlikely to default on rental payments and once ensconced are unwilling to move their offices because of the huge disruption this causes.

Upward only rent reviews

One of the greatest inventions of the UK commercial property market is the upward only rent review. Every five years or so the rent to be paid by the tenant on the property is renegotiated, if necessary by bringing in some form of arbitration, so the owner of the property can be assured of a continually rising income stream, hopefully to accompany a rising asset value. The over-supply problems of the early 1990s may have put a stop to the upward only rent review as more bargaining power was put in the hands of the occupiers, so any property portfolio with a collection of blue chip tenants on upward only rent reviews may now start to attract a premium from investors.

VALUATIONS

The established practice in the industry is to have the entire property portfolio revalued by an independent professional firm every year, but there can be cases in which the property is valued by the directors, who obviously have more optimistic valuations. In valuing some companies, especially developers, investors should be wary of capitalized costs, i.e. where the development costs and associated interest charges on debt are rolled up into the valuation of the property company. This is fine if the property is eventually realized for the value anticipated, but can leave substantial shortfalls otherwise. Analysts generally prefer to see costs written off as they occur, not least because it makes the valuation of the company easier.

Net asset values

The crucial tool for valuing property companies is the Net Asset Value (NAV) per share. As with all market valuations, investors are concerned not with the historic figure but what it is most likely to be at the next balance sheet date. It is very unlikely for a property company's share price to exceed its NAV, unless substantial growth in the portfolio value is expected.

Discount to NAV

Virtually all property stocks trade at a discount to their NAV. The reason for this is that investors have no control over the asset, and with larger companies do not even know what is in the portfolio from one day to the next.

That said, the whole rationale for investing in property companies is similar to that of investing in investment trusts. They produce greater portfolio diversity than direct property holdings and are managed by experts.

As the NAV per share fluctuates on an annual basis (with the year end valuation) and forecasts of its likely performance on a daily basis, so does the discount to NAV. This reflects both the mechanics of the market in balancing buyers and sellers but also investors' perceptions of the attractiveness of property as an investment.

Therefore the discount to NAV of a new issue is crucial. This should be compared with similar stocks in the sector bearing in mind portfolio distribution, but must be attractive in order for the stock to have any chance to perform. A new issue priced at a small discount to NAV has to grow its portfolio value in order to see its share price perform (this applies in the longer term to all stocks, of course), but one priced at a generous discount to NAV offers the prospect of short-term gains as well.

OFFICE/COMMERCIAL/RETAIL

The prospectus should give details of the property portfolio and a breakdown of the respective holdings of office, commercial and retail property. All can have their attractions, but office property on long-term lease to a high quality tenant is often considered a better investment. Commercial property is considered to have fewer high quality tenants with greater propensity to default, and returns from retail property can be volatile, depending on the fortunes of the retail market to fill the voids in the high streets and shopping centres. However, FT-SE 100 quoted company Land Securities is also one of the largest owners of shopping centres in the country.

FREEHOLD/LONG LEASEHOLD/
SHORT LEASEHOLD

Freehold property, which the owner owns in perpetuity, is obviously considered a better investment than other forms of tenure. Long leasehold, where the owner has rights over the property for a period of 100 years or more, is effectively the same from the point of view of property investment, but short leasehold is another matter. Leases which only have a few years left to run obviously reduce the returns on the property to investors, and can also discourage potential long-term tenants.

DIVIDEND YIELD

Property stocks (but not developers) are traditionally high yielders compared with the market as a whole, in part because they are considered an alternative to direct property investment by institutions. As the smaller institutions at least appear to be moving out of direct property into property stocks, pressure may even increase for high dividend payouts.

While a normal trading company might be comfortable with dividend cover of twice or more, it is common for property stocks to pay out the bulk of their earnings as dividend.

It is common for property stocks to pay out the bulk of their earnings as dividend.

High dividend yields can only be supported if the company is making sufficient profits to support them. These profits come in the form of rental income. Property companies do of course realize profits from the sale of investments, but these are not regarded as recurring or predictable items, so the dividend should be capable of being paid out of rental income less overheads. It should also be above the market average unless there are reasons to the contrary in the prospectus. For this reason the absence of a dividend forecast in a property company issue begs some questions.

CHECKLIST

i   *Is the company an investment or development company (Development can ring some alarm bells, but look at Chelsfield.) What is the proportion of development property in its portfolio? Are any costs capitalized?*

ii *Quality of covenant. Are there any recognizable names as tenants? What is the proportion of freehold/long leasehold/short leasehold? What percentage is unoccupied?*

iii *What is the discount to NAV (historic and any brokers' forecasts)?*

iv *What is the yield? Does it stack up with others in the sector?*

v   *Can the yield be supported out of rental income rather than disposal profits?*

'Greater portfolio diversity to the smaller investor.'

9

INVESTMENT TRUSTS
AND WARRANTS

- Investment and unit trusts
- Portfolio diversity
- Investment in otherwise difficult shares/markets
- Different types of shares
- Discount to net asset value
- Warrants

WHY BUY INVESTMENT TRUSTS?

The greatest problem associated with investment trusts from a new issues viewpoint is their tendency to go to a discount in early trading compared with the issue price. So why is it that so many investment trust new issues are successfully digested by the market each year. The answer is that an investment trust can offer greater portfolio diversity to the smaller investor, investment expertise in a particular sector or market and exposure to a market which otherwise would be closed to many, for instance the emerging markets of Asia.

The attractions of investing at the start include the fact that no commission is payable (a first day discount of 2 per cent is probably equivalent to paying spread plus commission) and some investment trusts can be tightly held, leading to illiquid markets.

THE DIFFERENCE BETWEEN A UNIT TRUST AND AN INVESTMENT TRUST

The crucial difference between these two types of collective investment scheme is the way they are valued. A unit trust is valued by taking the asset value of all of the fund's investments and dividing by the total number of units in issue. This is modified by the manager's decision as to whether to be on an offer or a bid basis, depending on the balance of buying and selling interest, and the dealing spread.

These factors notwithstanding, the value of the units in a unit trust fluctuate broadly in line with the value of the fund's underlying investments, and any new investors after the issue will get in at roughly net asset value. Further discussion of the unit trust market is beyond the scope of this book, not least because of the simplicities of valuation, and the fact that dealing is generally done through the fund's own managers.

> An investment trust . . . derives all or virtually all its income and capital gains from holdings in other quoted and unquoted companies.

An investment trust is similarly a collective investment scheme, but it is constituted as, and quoted as, a company. It has directors and publishes accounts, but the crucial difference between it and any other company listed on the stock market is that it derives all or virtually all its income and capital gains from holdings in other quoted and unquoted companies.

But it is important to realize that a quoted investment trust does not necessarily invest in quoted investments. To satisfy current legislation, an investment trust must invest 85 per cent of its funds in quoted stocks.

In this respect 3i (Investors in Industry, now a FT-SE 100 company) can be likened to an investment trust as its main activity is the taking of equity stakes in unquoted companies to provide venture capital. The difference between 3i and an investment trust is that it also lends money to these companies, which an investment trust does not.

THE LEGAL DEFINITION

Strictly, an investment trust is an investment scheme which has been approved of by the Inland Revenue as an investment trust for the purposes of section 842 of the Income and Corporation Taxes Act 1988 in respect of its most recent accounting period. Investment trust status has some valuable tax benefits in terms of both income and corporation tax. A trust can lose its investment trust status if it turns into an investment dealing company, or becomes a close company (with very few shareholders), or becomes a normal trading company. This can happen, as small investment trusts can be very useful 'shell companies' for a reverse takeover.

VALUING AN INVESTMENT TRUST

Because virtually all of the assets of an investment trust consist of holdings in other companies, it is relatively easy in most cases to value the company. The most important valuation criteria for an investment trust is the net asset value per share, which is calculated by taking the sum total of the trust's holdings, less any debt (trusts may be allowed to borrow), and dividing by the number of shares in issue. The crucial point about the NAV per share is that there are very few circumstances in which a trust will trade at a premium to its NAV, so this can be regarded as the effective maximum share price at any given time (for exceptions see below).

What's the problem with net asset values?

Almost all investment trusts trade at a discount to their NAV/ share. This is because investment trusts are quoted companies and the actual share price depends on the level of buying and selling interest through the market makers of the trust's shares. If there are more sellers than buyers (a traditional dealer's response to enquiries as to why shares are going down) the stock price will fall, regardless of the NAV.

However, if the price falls below a certain level the market will either start to consider the shares cheap, or the managers of the trust will use their powers to buy back some of the shares in the market, enhancing the net asset value of those remaining. Similarly, if the price exceeds the net asset value, investors will conclude, all other things being equal, that they could buy the same assets more cheaply directly in the market.

Managers take their costs out

All collective investment schemes must in aggregate underperform the market or index against which they are measured, because their managers take their fees out of the income of the fund. Therefore the total value of the assets of the fund

> **The total value of the assets of the fund will always be eroded by the fees of the fund managers.**

will always be eroded by the fees of the fund managers. But this is not the real reason why investment trusts trade at a discount to their net asset value. The primary reason is control. Property companies trade at a discount to net asset value because the investors do not have control over the acquisition and disposal of the assets of the company, and the same is true of investment trusts.

In the case of an investment trust, not only do investors not have control over the buying and selling of the assets of the trust (although they can collectively fire the managers at an EGM of the fund), but they also do not know what all the assets are for most of the year. The fund managers must disclose the 20 largest holdings with the accounts, and publish the NAV per share with the interim and final results, but the holdings of the fund do not have to be disclosed in minute detail and can of course change from one day to the next.

Discount to net asset value

In practice, investment trusts generally trade at a discount to NAV of 0–30 per cent. It is this fluctuation which determines the day to day share price as much as the six monthly NAV update. However,

investors and analysts do make forecasts of prospective NAV performance based on the known holdings of the funds and
performance of the various market sectors. Investment trusts tend
to act like other derivatives of the equity market. When prices are
going up the discount to NAV narrows, not least because buying
into a trust can be a more effective way of gaining exposure to a
sector in one go, and when prices are falling they fall further than
the underlying market as the discount widens.

The market virtually always applies a discount to the value of
something which it cannot control. The reverse of this situation is
evident if another company chooses to make a takeover bid for an
investment trust, a form of disguised rights issue if the holdings
are later liquidated. Holders of the trust's shares will generally
only sell out at net asset value.

SO WHAT DOES THIS MEAN FOR THE NEW ISSUE MARKET?

In essence, the tendency of an investment trust to trade at a discount to its NAV means that most investment trust new issues
should trade at a discount to the price at which investors apply.
The total value of the fund is set by the number and size of applications, but the discount for lack of control will always apply. So
why bother to invest in an investment trust new issue rather than
buying the stock in the market later – and cheaper?

Different types of shares and derivatives

There can be reasons to buy at issue rather than in the aftermarket
because of problems of liquidity, as some investment trusts can be
very tightly held. But the main reason is that investment managers
and sponsors have become very aware of the problems attendant
to an investment trust new issue and nearly always introduce
derivatives on the share price to erode the discount.

This can involve different types of shares with different entitlements to participation in the gains in asset value as the underlying

investments perform (split capital and income shares), but this must be a zero sum game in aggregate. The most common form of equity kicker is now the warrant issue.

UK Investment Trusts with a Public Offer Element 1994

Trust	Method	Proceeds (£m)
Abtrust High Income	O/Sub @ 100p	30.5
Baring Emerging Europe	O/Sub & PL @ US$1	82.7
BZW Commodities	O/Sub & PL @ 100p	78.2
Central European Growth	O/Sub & PL @ US$1	134.7
Edinburgh Inca	O/Sub @ 50p	100.0
Edinburgh New Tiger	O/Sub @ 50p	110.0
Fidelity Japanese Values	O/Sub & PL @ 100p	105.3
Fidelity Special Values	O/Sub @ 100p	45.5
Fleming Indian	O/Sub & PL @ 100p	84.0
Fleming Natural Resources	O/Sub & PL @ 100p	41.0
Foreign & Colonial Inc Growth	O/Sub & PL @ 100p	250.0
Gartmore British Inc & Growth	O/Sub @ 100p	108.0
Gartmore Micro Index	O/Sub & PL @ 100p	35.5
Govett Global Smaller Cos	O/Sub & PL @ 100p	21.7
International Biotechnology	O/Sub & PL @ 100p	37.7
INVESCO Japan Discovery	O/Sub @ 100p	27.9
Israel Fund	O/Sub & PL @ US$1	102.2
Johnson Fry European Utilities	O/Sub @ 100p	15.0
Kleinwort Euro Privatisation	O/Sub & PL @ 100p	500.0
Legal & General Recovery	O/Sub @ 100p	36.8
Mercury Euro Privatisation	IO & O/Sub & PL @ 100p	575.0
Morgan Grenfell Latin American	O/Sub @ 100p	125.0
Murray Emerging Economies	O/Sub @ 100p	65.0
Old Mutual South Africa	IO & PL @ 100p	70.0
Piper European Smaller Cos	O/Sub & PL @ 100p	27.0
Prolific Income	O/Sub @ 100p	51.8
Saracen Value	IO & PL @ 100p	37.0
Schroder Japan Growth	O/Sub & PL @ 100p	125.0
Schroder UK Growth	O/Sub @ 100p	117.2
Schroder Latin American	IO & PL @ 100p	50.1
Templeton Latin American	O/Sub & PL @ 100p	46.2
Undervalued Assets	O/Sub @ 100p	60.0

Key O/Sub: Offer for subscription
PL: Placing
IO: Intermediaries offer

UK Investment Trust Placings in 1994

Trust	Price	Proceeds (£m)
Abtrust Latin American	100p	20.0
Baronsmead	100p	12.8
Beacon	100p	19.0
First Russian Frontiers	US$10	35.8
Foreign & Colonial Private Equity	100p	25.0
Guangdong Development	US$1	61.6
Hambros Smaller Asian Cos	US$1	26.4
Herald	100p	65.0
Hoare Govett 1000 Index	100p	30.0
Matheson Lloyds	100p	25.0
Mithras	50p	20.0
Oryx	US$10.30	17.0
Prospect Japan	US$10.30	49.5
Taiwan	100p	45.0

WARRANTS

A warrant is similar to a traded option in that it gives the right to buy shares at a predetermined price and time in the future. However, it differs from a traded option in that the right is exercisable against the company, which issues new shares to satisfy the warrant exercise, whereas in the case of an option exercise, only existing shares are delivered.

Warrants also differ from traded options in that they are usually exercisable (at certain windows of opportunity) for between three and seven years, sometimes longer, compared with the six months' duration of a traded option.

Why do companies issue warrants? On the face of it there are few fundamental reasons to issue warrants from the point of view of the company, because the exercise price of the warrant is fixed so far in advance. If investors have paid for the warrant there is a benefit to the issuer if the share price never reaches the warrant's exercise price, but if the share price does perform very well there is the danger that the funds received by the company from the exercise price may be less as a proportion of the current share price than would be received had the company made a simple rights issue, and this would create some asset dilution. The problem in essence is that it is very difficult to predict several years ahead. However, a number of companies do choose to issue warrants, often as investor incentives. For a number of years BTR issued warrants free to existing investors.

However, warrants have some advantages for the investor, of which the most valuable is gearing. Depending on how aggressively the warrant is priced (i.e. how big a premium to the share price the exercise price is) a warrant can be very highly geared to movements in the value of the underlying share. A warrant with an exercise price just 20 per cent higher than the current share price and with five years to run will offer very few gearing advantages to straight equity as most investors in the stock would expect share price performance to be better than 20 per cent over five years, or they would probably not be holders. Therefore the warrant would be priced in the market at very close to the underlying equity and would move in line with it.

> **A number of companies . . . choose to issue warrants, often as investor incentives.**

Conversely, a warrant with an exercise price way in excess of the current share price with only a short time to expiry would be priced at a small percentage of the current share price and would increase in value significantly with any share price rise, as the chance of the exercise price being realized improved.

The main problem with warrants is that they are very hard to value because of their long exercise periods (up to seven years in some cases). Options are valued by most investors using the Black-Scholes model, which was derived as a mathematical formula from observations in the traded options market on the Chicago Board Options Exchange in the US, and are generally valid up to the longest date at which options are written: six months. The Black-Scholes model depends on measuring the historic volatility of movements in the share price of the stock in question, and from this derives a time value. If the stock has a high volatility, there is a greater chance that within the time for which the option runs the stock will rise to a point higher than the exercise price and make the option valuable.

There are two reasons why option pricing cannot easily be applied to warrants. One is that option pricing methods are usually applied only up to a duration of six months, the longest that a traded (rather than over the counter) option can run. Warrants are frequently issued with durations of seven years. The other is that option prices require highly liquid markets to be valid, something which is not always the case with warrant issues.

Some merchant banks do possess warrant pricing software but most investors are reduced to making a simple calculation and value judgement about a warrant. It is easy enough to calculate the premium to the current share price represented by the warrant's exercise price, and from that derive the compound growth in the share price required to make the warrant worth exercising before it expires and becomes worthless.

It is also worth making the point that as warrant pricing models require an estimate of volatility in the same way as options, most sophisticated pricing software is at a loss when considering a warrant accompanying a new issue, as there is no history of share price volatility.

Warrants are therefore very difficult for the market to value on an objective basis and tend to depend, as ultimately do all stocks, on the relative buying and selling interest in the market. This highlights one of the primary disadvantages of many warrant issues: liquidity is often poor due to the small size of the issue, resulting in very large spreads and small dealing sizes which make any gearing effects worthless. Often the only way to achieve the full value from many smaller company warrant issues is to hold them to term and exercise against the company, something which almost never happens in the traded options market.

Warrants have no shareholder rights or dividend entitlements

Because warrants are derivative instruments, holders do not in general have the rights of ordinary shareholders. This means they do not have the right to vote at EGMS or AGMS of the company (not a problem for private investors whose views are almost always overshadowed by the voting patterns of institutions), nor to receive dividends – a factor to be taken into account when valuing a warrant intended to be held beyond the next dividend date.

Gearing

Warrant issues are, however, valuable to both the company and to investors as they add value to an issue, even if mortgaging the future from the company's point of view. Investors receive an instrument which offers gearing to any share price performance of the company, which is of course the primary reason for investing in most new issues, and the company induces greater investment interest, especially where the warrants are packaged with ordinary equity, and not least because of the uncertain value of the warrant issue.

CHECKLIST

i   *Is the trust offering any geographical/portfolio diversity which cannot be obtained elsewhere?*

ii   *Is it offering any investment expertise not already possessed?*

iii *Will it have exposure to emerging markets or unquoted stocks which are otherwise unobtainable, expensive or risky?*

iv   *Are there different types of shares to be issued, e.g. split capital and income?*

v   *Is there a warrant package to offer some gearing?*

vi   *What is the level of flotation expenses and management fees?*

vii *Check the discount to NAV at which similar trusts are trading. Might it be possible to buy cheaper in the aftermarket?*

'Why do investors choose to put their money into foreign markets?'

10

ARE FOREIGN MARKETS ATTRACTIVE?

- ● **Why invest abroad?**
- ● **Getting in . . . and out**
- ● **Currency risks**
- ● **Emerging market funds**
- ● **Privatizations**
- ● **US IPO now the norm**

Is it worth the effort to invest in foreign new issues? The answer is a qualified yes, but only for the more sophisticated and larger investor. Dealing in foreign markets has a number of obvious and less apparent pitfalls. However, as securities markets become more global they are opening up more readily to outside investors and, in the case of some emerging markets, are keen to attract the huge investment funds of the Western World.

WHY INVEST ABROAD?

Why do investors choose to put their money into foreign markets when there are perfectly good opportunities at home? This question is especially relevant to UK pension funds, which have virtually all their liabilities in sterling and therefore should match them with most of their assets in sterling. Yet they choose to put in excess of 10 per cent of their funds into foreign markets. The simple answer is of course that they are hoping for exposure to markets with more growth potential. Almost all of the pension fund money in the world is tied up in North America and Europe, the countries which have the most ageing populations and the most mature domestic markets.

They are hoping for exposure to markets with more growth potential.

Economic growth in double figures is not only impossible to imagine in these countries, it would probably be considered undesirable. On the other hand, double-digit growth is being seen in several of the Asian 'Tiger' economies, and of course in China – the largest investment opportunity of the decade.

Growth markets

The stock markets of these countries offer growth opportunities not only because of the inherent economic growth of the economies they represent, but also because of the 'Wall of Money' trying to get into them. The amount of stock on offer in some of these markets is very small indeed and is being chased by vast investment funds from the West. The shortage of supply is exacerbated by the desire of domestic investors to participate in newly liberalized markets. But the sight of domestic private investors queuing up to invest in concepts they may only vaguely understand is not a comforting one – it has all the requirements for a market crash ('correction', in broker speak) when sentiment turns. Liquidity problems exacerbated the Wall Street crash.

GETTING IN . . . AND GETTING OUT

While there may be no commission costs on the way into a foreign new issue, although it is always wise to check, there can still be costs associated with the issue. For instance, it may not be possible under the investment laws of the country for an outside holder to own stock directly. It may be necessary, and indeed desirable, for the stock to be held in a nominee name and the custodian of the stock is perfectly entitled to charge an annual fee.

Bear in mind also that allocations can be, and usually are, biased in favour of domestic investors. This is true in the UK, where, in the recent privatization issues, foreign applicants were scaled down to satisfy UK retail applications. The same was true of the Renault privatization where UK applicants received less than 10 per cent of what they applied for in some cases. In these cases the adage of not wanting to be a member of any old club which would have you applies. Foreign investors, except the international banks, are usually at the bottom of the pile.

The biggest problem in dealing abroad is that commission charges are almost always higher, not least because most UK based clients need to deal through their own broker in the UK in the first instance. The UK broker will have a relationship with a broker in the market in question, but two lots of commission may be payable. Other markets are not as liquid as the UK, and not as over-broked, so competition may not have forced commission levels down.

However, liquidity can have much more serious consequences. Many overseas markets, especially the emerging markets, can suffer from severe liquidity problems which can mean it is effectively impossible to get out of a stock. This is true especially of order based dealing systems. Many emerging markets (and more developed ones as well) see all the business going 'one-way', that is either everybody is a buyer or everybody is a seller. If there is a severe order imbalance and no buyers can be found for the stock on offer, the shares can effectively be suspended. The UK system of market makers who are required to quote a live price all the time is supposed to eliminate this problem, but dealers attempting to hit a market maker with stock they do not want, know differently.

Many emerging markets . . . see all the business going 'one-way'.

CURRENCIES

Investors in foreign markets are soon taught a simple lesson. It is perfectly possible for a huge profit to be made on a stock in the local currency as the domestic market soars, only to lose the lot as the currency depreciates against sterling. The reverse can be true in that the stock can fail to perform at all but still make money on currency appreciation. As foreign exchange markets can be very volatile, however, it is better to leave currency speculation to professionals. Investors will also lose a small turn when converting into currency to go in and get out of the investment, although the spreads charged are in general far smaller than those charged for tourist foreign exchange.

Dividends

However, the problem of currency translation becomes serious when it comes to dividends. Most banks charge a punitive rate for cashing a cheque received in a foreign currency, to the point where any income from a foreign equity is eroded completely. There can also be withholding taxes in the overseas market which hit income, and there may be no double taxation agreement between the authorities and the Inland Revenue to allow for foreign tax.

QUALITY OF INFORMATION

The UK has probably the most sophisticated and efficient systems for the dissemination of financial information in the world, beating even the US for ease of access. UK investors and analysts are often confounded by the inaccessibility of basic financial information even within Europe, let alone in the more esoteric emerging markets where accounting standards may be substantially different. The consequence of this is that information on which an investment decision might be based, which may be available as a matter of course in the UK, may simply not be available in overseas markets. This state of affairs applies even to the best of the professionals in a market.

For the private client it can be virtually impossible to discover what is going on. As information is not necessarily disseminated to all parties at once (to be fair this applies just as much in the UK on occasion) private investors from overseas can be sure they will be the last to know about some impending disaster and the last to be able to get out. They are in the position of the famous Japanese Housewife – used to bail somebody else out of a bad position. In all financial markets information is passed on down the line according to how important the recipient is to the person in the know. Large clients are always called first.

EMERGING MARKET FUNDS

Unit trusts, investment trusts and other collective investment are worth considering in relation to overseas new issues. In fact there are some funds created specifically to invest in overseas new issues, such as the Kleinwort European Privatisation Fund, and some which offer opportunities to invest in markets where direct investment is simply impossible. There are, for instance, several Vietnam funds, when for most UK based investors it would be inadvisable, if not impossible, to invest in Vietnam. It is fair to say, however, that even these funds can find it difficult to invest in their markets and can be forced either to sit on large amounts of cash waiting for the opportunity, or they invest in companies in more accessible markets which do business in the country in question. This is not quite the same as direct investment. Because of the structure and investment policy of these funds some are marketed solely to investment professionals.

Mexico was one of the darlings of the emerging markets economies in the early 1990s. The country was seen to be maturing politically, had economic and political stability and, more importantly, bordered on the continental United States. It was seen as the logical route for investment in lower cost manufacturing, and when membership of the North American Free Trade Agreement loomed, it seemed too good to be true. Just as important, the Mexican finance ministry was staffed with ex-Harvard students who spoke the same language as their potential investors, both literally and in terms of economic objectives.

A privatization programme was instituted and the stocks were heavily and slickly marketed in London and Europe as well as the

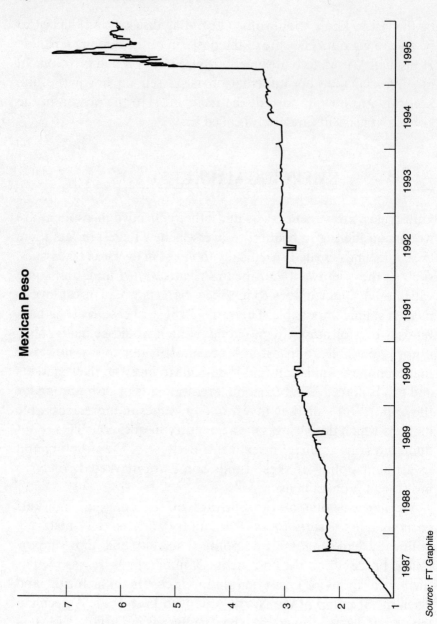

Mexican Peso

Source: FT Graphite

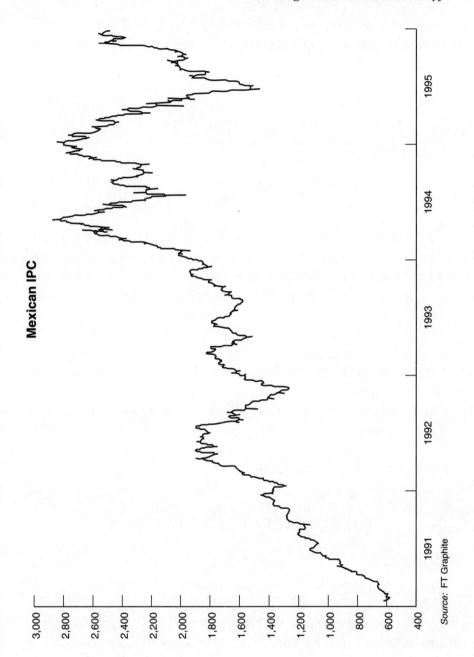

Mexican IPC

Source: FT Graphite

United States. Early issues did indeed go well, but the rapid down-turn in the economy and market crash precipitated by the austerity programme in early 1995 left many overseas investors stunned. Not only did the market fall by several percentage points, but trading was halted for several days. Overseas investors were also hit by the currency's depreciation against the dollar. Getting out in these circumstances was next to impossible.

PRIVATIZATIONS

There is very little left to privatize in the UK but Margaret Thatcher's legacy to the stock markets of the world, and many grateful brokers, is the drive to privatization. Not only are privatization programmes in train in the developed countries of Europe (with Deutsche Telekom and the French privatization of its auto-motive and tobacco industries), but the former Soviet Union and Eastern Bloc countries have also leaped at the idea. Dealing in these issues in the East will be very difficult for some time, but the countries with the most advanced programmes are those of Latin America. The region is no longer the economic basket case it was over a decade ago, (Mexican debacle notwithstanding) and infla-tion, once the bugbear of these countries, is in some cases lower than in some European counterparts.

THE US MARKET FOR NEW ISSUES

Investing in new issues in the US can be very disconcerting for investors brought up in the UK because their well-founded in-clination to submit applications at the last minute is counter-productive. The system in the US is designed to produce early indications of interest and those submitting their applications at the last minute are more than likely to be considered stags and cut out of the process. They may often find that they are too late because offers can be closed early if quality applications for enough stock have been received.

Furthermore, the price is often not fixed until the very last minute and investors are expected, it seems, to trust to the pricing instincts of the house running the issue. This runs counter to most of the instincts of the UK fund manager, but the system does work well from the point of view of the vendor. The book building process ascertains the level of genuine investment interest for any given pricing level, and the 'Green Shoe' and stabilization both enable the aftermarket to be managed. The system has recently been imported into the UK for several large issues including BT3, the Gencos issue and BSkyB, and the net effect would seem to be that it makes stagging the issue less profitable.

US-style IPOs

The annual crop of new issues on the New York Stock Exchange (NYSE) and NASDAQ (National Association of Securities Dealers) dwarfs that of other world stock markets. In 1993 the NYSE alone saw 219 issues, both domestic and overseas stocks, and raised $46.6bn. Nearly half this sum comprised overseas listings.

The US model for handling new issues, known as Initial Public Offerings (IPO), has accordingly become the norm for emerging markets as the issuers seek wherever possible to mimic US reporting styles to make their issues more attractive to US investment funds.

This has also increasingly been the case with new issues in developed markets as larger issues become global in nature. Consequently the US method of marketing an IPO is now standard. The roadshow followed by indications of interest has now largely replaced fixed price offers for sale for larger UK issues and the same is noticeable in continental European markets. US developments, such as stabilization and the Green Shoe option, are also now commonplace on larger issues.

ADR/GDR TRADING

Another consequence of the move to attract funds on a global basis is the increased use of ADR/GDR trading (American/Global

Depositary Receipts) on international markets.

To help alleviate the difficulties in trading in some markets, the stocks are now traded in an internationally accepted form on certain exchanges. ADRs merely represent a receipt for the underlying stock held by a bank's global custody department. Rather than trading the underlying security which may have settlement problems in its home market, international traders trade the ADR instead.

> **The stocks are now traded in an internationally accepted form on certain exchanges.**

The great advantage of an ADR listing is that investors can trade in the stock either in their home market or in a market more familiar to them such as Wall Street or London. SEAQ International in London has become so successful that even certain European stocks are more liquid on SEAQ than they are in their domestic market.

CHECKLIST

- *Where are the shares listed – is there an ADR/GDR traded preferably in the US or UK as well as a local listing? The ADR/GDR can be more liquid.*

- *What is liquidity like in the local market?*

- *Are there restrictions on share ownership/transfer?*

- *What are the dealing costs and settlement details?*

- *Are there any custody charges?*

- *How are dividends paid to overseas holders – are there withholding taxes?*

- *Bear in mind the currency exposure*

- *Is information on the market and company easily available?*

'The great
advantage of
the PEP is the
opportunity to
avoid tax'.

11

SOME FURTHER CONSIDERATIONS

- Are new issues getting younger?
- Is there a season?
- PEP schemes
- Smaller companies and market capitalizations
- Prices and commissions
- Does the share price matter?

ARE NEW ISSUES GETTING YOUNGER?

Anecdotal evidence suggests that the market is now prepared to invest in companies at an earlier stage of development than had been the case in previous generations. This is obvious in the number of management buyouts which return to the market sometimes just months after the MBO, but also in the trading history of other stocks seeking a listing.

The Unlisted Securities Market (USM) (closed to new entrants, and soon to cease to exist completely) was created to allow companies without the required trading history access to a market quote, and the Stock Exchange has introduced new rules to cater for scientific research based companies. But it seems that companies looking for a perfectly standard full listing are also getting younger and are coming to the market with trading histories which would have made earlier generations of institutional fund managers decidedly nervous.

An example of the new shift in the market came in early 1995 with the flotation (via placing in both cases) of Vision Group and Rainford. Rainford was unusual and received a great deal of press coverage because it was not a management buyout but had been founded nearly 20 years previously by its present chief executive with just £1,500. On flotation his stake was worth several million pounds. The issue was worthy of note because the apparent conventional nature of its history had by then become unusual

By comparison, Vision Group came to the market at the very first opportunity. The stock was placed at a price which capitalized the company at £30m. It did have a revenue earning operation employing 47 people, but its products were at a very early stage of development; revenue in the year prior to flotation was less than £1m. A valuation of 30 times sales, the only reasonable measure as the company was almost inevitably not profitable, is demanding by virtually any comparison. Nevertheless, investors were keen to get their hands on more technology based stocks after recent profitable experience and the placing was easily done. Vision Group had been founded in 1990 and had a number of exciting products developed from a low cost chip based camera. It must have only just satisfied the Stock Exchange rules for a full listing. Investors did not seem to care, but wanted to get in on the ground floor of what was perceived to be a high growth stock.

They offer investors the chance to gain exposure to high growth stocks at an earlier point in their development.

It would seem that issues of this sort are more and more likely to be the norm. They offer investors the chance to gain exposure to high growth stocks at an earlier point in their development, giving some the chance to participate in what might turn out to be the new Microsoft. On the other hand, investors will no longer be able to assume that, merely because a company has a full listing, it is something of substance. More judgement in investing in these issues will be required. There has been considerable press coverage of the likely dangers of investing in the new AIM market, but it would seem that there are not as many differences between that and the full market as some might suppose.

IS THERE A SEASON?

'Sell in May and go away' is an old market adage about the lack of business seen in the market during the summer months and the consequent likely fall in the market. The usefulness of such simplistic rules as an investment tool is limited, but there is some seasonality in the new issues market. In part this reflects the seasonality of the market as a whole – and finding the more senior managers in the investment community can be difficult in high summer as the attractions of sporting events and school holidays beckon – but also two factors of specific relevance.

The first is the end of the tax year on 5 April and the consequent flood of money into PEP schemes to beat the deadline (issues straddling the end of the tax year by a few weeks can qualify for two PEP schemes). Out of 130 of the largest issues of the last two years, March was the most popular month to bring an issue to the market with 22 issues impacting in that month.

The second factor is flows in institutional and personal cash flow. This is of little importance for smaller new issues targeted at both institutions and more sophisticated investors, but it would be counter-productive on the part of the sponsors of a major public offer to hit the market at a time when the general public feels short of cash. This means avoiding Christmas and the summer holidays, when investors have other things on their minds. In the years 1993 and 1994 there were just four issues in August and September combined and none in January.

For much the same reasons, individual investors' saving decisions impact the flow of funds to institutions running unit trusts and similar products. For a multiplicity of reasons, therefore, the second and fourth quarters of the year are the most attractive for both sponsors and investors after taking into account the PEP distortion in March, leading to a scramble to the market in the event of sentiment picking up.

New issues (over £25m) in 1993 and 1994, by month

January	0
February	8
March	22
April	7
May	16
June	21
July	11
August	3
September	1
October	9
November	23
December	10

Amount raised by new issues, 1993 and 1994

Half year	Mkt cap
H1 1993	£1.678bn
H2 1993	£3.296bn
H1 1994	£5.511bn
H2 1994	£3.375bn

Source: James Capel

PEP SCHEMES

UK Personal Equity Plans (PEPs) are very popular with the sponsors of new issues as they represent private client investment funds which are, unusually, not short term in their objectives.

Much of the stock applied for in new issues by the general public comes back on to the market in the first weeks of trading if there is a profit to be realized. Stock held through PEP schemes, on the other hand, is largely locked in for the long term and provides a stable investor base. Sponsors make considerable efforts to ensure that issues are attractive to PEP managers. The timing of the National Power/PowerGen flotation in early 1995 was arranged near the end of the tax year partly to ensure that the stock could be put in the PEP schemes of two different years.

Any individual may start one general and one single company PEP in each tax year. The maximum amount which can be put into a general PEP is £6,000, while for a single company PEP it is £3,000.

A general PEP can invest in a wide variety of individual shares and collective investment schemes, but given the relatively small size of the funds originally invested, the number of investments is usually kept small, helping to keep charges down. A single company PEP, a more recent invention, can only invest in the shares of one company. Some companies now offer to administer these for investors themselves hoping to retain a loyal small shareholder base.

There are restrictions as to what shares are eligible for PEP schemes and a limit on the investment in unit trust funds. PEP schemes are either run by fund managers, in which case they invest primarily in the funds of that institution, or they can be 'self select' PEPs where the investor decides in which shares the scheme will invest. The entire £6,000 of a general PEP scheme can also be invested in a single stock, making it possible to invest £9,000 in the shares of a single company through the two schemes in any one year. At this point the tax advantages of the PEP can start to become significant when applied to certain new issues.

> **Stock held through PEP schemes . . . is largely locked in for the long term and provides a stable investor base.**

The great advantage of the Personal Equity Plan is the opportunity to avoid tax, both income tax on dividends and capital gains on share price appreciation. All individuals in the UK have a capital gains tax threshold which means that currently the first £5,000 of gains on shares is tax free, but dividend income received into a PEP is also tax free. This is of value to all taxpayers, but especially to those paying higher rate tax.

However, it is not universally the case that stock acquired in a new issue should automatically be put in a PEP, especially if it means the exclusion of other equity holdings. PEP managers charge entry and exit fees, and also charge an annual management fee. This fee has to come out of the income of the PEP scheme, and its only income comes in the form of dividends.

Many new issues are growth stocks with below average or nominal yields, as befits a company which is retaining all its cash to fund growth. In this case the tax saved on the dividend income may not offset the charges levied by the PEP manager so there would be little point in having the stock in the PEP scheme. Put something with a higher yield in instead.

However, there are some new issues which come to the market with an above average yield. In these cases the income advantages can be considerable. It would not be impossible for certain types of ex-growth stocks to have a yield of in excess of 6 per cent gross, compared with around 4.5 per cent for the market as a whole. On a figure of £6,000 invested this means an initial saving before management charges of £144 a year for a higher rate taxpayer, and this yield is of course likely to rise in subsequent years.

But the greatest yield advantage of PEP schemes in new issues comes with partly paid stocks. Partly paid stocks offer greater gearing to increases in the capital value of stocks, but in most cases are also entitled to dividend income on the same basis as the fully paid stock. In the case of recent privatizations when stock had to be paid for in three instalments with around a third payable on application, investors saw a gross yield approaching 20 per cent on their partly paid stock first instalment. This advantage declines of course as the second and third calls have to be paid, but the yield and consequent tax saving through a PEP scheme become considerable in year one.

Many new issue prospectuses for offers for sale now include specific provisions for PEP allocations whereby the application form signals that the stock is destined for a PEP scheme. In other cases the holder of a stock bought in a new issue has 42 days (six weeks) to put the stock in the PEP scheme. This is done through the PEP manager.

Are there any drawbacks to PEP schemes?

In addition to entry and exit fees, PEP schemes usually have an annual management charge with a minimum fee. Charges reduce as a proportion of the sum invested as the sum gets closer to the £6,000 or £3,000 limit. Charges for single company PEPs can be lower.

Investors in new issues cannot be sure of how much stock they will be allocated, although in some new issues preference is given to PEP applications. But in the case of heavily oversubscribed issues, often the ones with the partly paid income advantages, allocations can be a small proportion of the stock applied for. This can mean that charges make it unprofitable to put the stock in a PEP at all, or force the PEP manager to top up at a potentially higher price in the aftermarket.

Stock held in PEP schemes is almost without exception held in nominee names for ease of administration. This denies the shareholder the right to vote at AGMs (most do not bother anyway) and also means that they will not be on the mailing list for a copy of the annual accounts and other communications from the company. More importantly, the shareholder incentives in some new issues, such as bonus shares for those who hold the stock for three years or so, apply only to individual holders. Nominee accounts do not qualify for the payouts.

ARE SMALLER COMPANIES MORE ATTRACTIVE?

The market capitalization of a company (i.e. the aggregate value of its shares in issue) is important not only because it dictates by what means it can come to the market, but also because it affects who will invest in the stock. Most fund managers attempt to limit the number of stocks they hold, if only for ease of administration, and therefore treat 'smaller companies' as a distinct category. These are often managed by a separate smaller companies fund manager. There is no accepted definition of a smaller company, but for most investment managers it will be a company with a market capitalization of less than £100m or £50m.

There are sound reasons for the distinction, because institutions deal in such large quantities of stock. While a unit trust may be satisfied with a minimum holding of £100,000 in any one stock (£250,000 is more likely), pension funds tend to hold millions of pounds worth of any one stock, and any smaller scraps are regularly culled from the funds. If a fund has a multiplicity of holdings, it becomes very difficult for the fund managers to get a grip on why their fund is or is not performing.

Even if performing very well, a tiny holding is unlikely to make much difference to the fund performance.

And even if performing very well, a tiny holding is unlikely to make much difference to the fund performance.

There is another very relevant distinction between smaller companies and others, from an institutional point of view. Because institutions like to get hold of a relatively large slug of stock, one fund can end up as one of the largest holders of a company's stock, and sometimes with a declarable stake, especially if it has a market capitalization in the £25m range.

This means in turn that it is very difficult to get out as it may not be easy to find a buyer for the stake, and the fund manager is in much more for the long term. In this respect the smaller companies fund manager has to develop a much closer relationship with the company and its management, more akin to venture capital than conventional fund management.

MARKET CAPITALIZATIONS

The market capitalization of a stock determines whether it will be included in any of the market indices, and in turn influences who will cover the stock. A company large enough to get into the FT-SE 100 will be covered by analysts from virtually every major stockbroking firm, and will receive extensive press coverage of all its results and deals. Similarly, the same applies to S&P 500 (Standard & Poors) stocks in the US.

At the other end of the scale, a company with a capitalization of £5m may only be covered by the broker which brought it to the market and may struggle to get a mention in the *Financial Times* or the *Investors Chronicle*.

Market capitalizations and indices are relevant to the new issues investor because of the existence of 'tracking' funds. Investors have woken up to the fact that because they take charges out of the funds they manage, average fund managers must underperform the index they are measured against. Recent years have seen the advent of passively managed tracking funds which seek only to track the value of the index they are measured against. The most common of these is the FT-SE 100, but others exist. If a new market entrant is likely to be included in the FT-SE 100 the market generally concludes that index funds will buy it. Hence healthy demand is expected.

The FT-SE 100 index is the index of the leading 100 stocks in the UK by market capitalization (the total value of all the shares in issue). Membership of the FT-SE 100 is reviewed every three months by the steering committee and those stocks which have underperformed significantly are replaced by stocks which have reached the threshold.

This, incidentally, is why the FT-SE 100 should outperform the market as a whole. The steering committee exercises some judgement so at any one time a stock which is, say, 107th by capitalization could well be in the index. Note also that free float matters. Waste Management International has a large enough market capitalization to get into the index, but because only 25 per cent of the shares are freely held in the UK it is excluded. The FT-SE 100 is the subject of so much interest because trading in FT-SE stocks accounts for around 50 per cent of market turnover, and the index accounts for around half the total UK market capitalization.

In 1995 a stock needed a market capitalization of around £1.8bn to be included in the FT-SE 100. The relatively recent Mid 250 index is the index of the next largest 250 companies, with a minimum capitalization of around £300m, and finally there is the All-Share index. Another index of relevance to the new issue investor is the Hoare Govett Smaller Companies Index, into which many new issues will fall. It demonstrates the advantages – at times – of investing in smaller companies.

'THERE IS NO COMMISSION ON NEW ISSUES'

One of the apparent attractions of investing in new issues is that there is no broker's commission to be paid on the way in. This is not true – it is merely concealed in the offer price. In intermediaries offers brokers are more often than not paid a kick-back of around 1 per cent (although in some cases it can be as high as 4 per cent) on the total value of clients' applications accepted. This gives them some incentive to handle the intermediaries offer business, for otherwise they would only see some income from the offer when the stock was subsequently sold. One of the reasons for the relatively lukewarm interest in the General Cable issue, which was pulled first time around and second time had its price reduced to 190 pence from 220-255 pence, was that no commission was paid to intermediaries. But does this mean that brokers are less than impartial in judging new issues? It should not, because the more intelligent ones realize that decent clients deal quite regularly and one bad deal can put them off for a while.

DOES THE SHARE PRICE MATTER?

The share price at which a new issue comes to the market should not make any difference, but it does. All shares should be valued on criteria such as earnings or net asset value per share, or yield, all of which enable one share to be compared with another. The fact that one stock can have a share price ten times larger than another is, or should be, irrelevant.

However, there is a well-founded perception in the UK market that the absolute price of a share does have some effect on the willingness of investors to buy it. Few companies in the UK have a share price of over 500 pence, and when the price gets to this level the company will often subdivide the shares to bring the price down. This does not affect the value of the holding of any existing shareholders, of course. They merely have, say, two shares worth 250 pence when previously they had one worth 500 pence. However, this simply does not apply in the US and most other markets, and US share prices are much higher than those in the UK. Absolute prices say nothing about value, but UK retail investors are put off by high prices.

The reason for this is the private client's interest in capital appreciation. It should be patently obvious that the value of a share will increase in line with the consensus of the stock's asset value or prospects, but many investors perceive that they have a chance of faster capital appreciation with 'penny' shares than those with a price measured in pounds. In one respect they are right in that a penny share price often indicates a company which has been in trouble and could therefore be a recovery situation. But it can also mean that it is on the verge of going into liquidation. For this reason any new issue priced in single figures might raise some questions as to how it got to that level in the first place.

New issuers capitalize on this perception. Most issues come to the market with a share price in the region of 100 pence (a round figure) or higher, but less than £10. US attitudes to price are different. Stock prices of $20 to $50 are the norm. This can be manipulated by changing the number of shares issued. But some new issues come with a penny share price. Are these issuers saying something to the market? It could be that they are trying to appeal to the penny share investor, with a subliminal message that the share price is set to rise very quickly.

For there are in fact some disadvantages of a low share price. The first is another market anomaly which strictly speaking should not exist. But it is the case that the market maker's spread on penny shares is higher than on others. This is primarily a consequence of the low liquidity of many of these smaller stocks, but also results from rounding. Market makers will generally only quote down to a quarter penny at the minimum, although they may deal at any price. For most issues, unless they are trading very actively, the spread will be a penny, perhaps representing a spread of more than 10 per cent. It is, of course, up to the broker doing the deal to negotiate a better price, but on the face of it spreads are higher for penny stocks.

Another point to bear in mind with penny shares is that it is not possible under English company law to issue shares at a discount to par value (par value is of virtually no relevance for the new issue investor). This is an historical anomaly but presents a problem for companies whose share price has fallen below par value. The shares then generally have to be subdivided, some cancelled, and High Court approval sought for the capital reorganization. This is unlikely to apply to most new issues, but can be highly relevant to reverse takeovers of shell companies.

'Stags have missed
an opportunity for
greater profit in the
long term.'

12

FIRST DAY PREMIUMS
AND STAGGING

- ● **The first day premium**
- ● **Why do stocks go to a premium?**
- ● **Institutions and private investors**
- ● **Over- and under-subscription**
- ● **Is stagging worth it?**
- ● **Gearing up**
- ● **The Grey Market**

FIRST DAY PREMIUMS

The ultimate intention of the sponsor in the new issue process is to manage the debut of the company on the stock market in such a way that both vendors and investors feel they have done well out of the deal. In simple terms this boils down to a first day premium to the issue price. Sentiment is hugely important in the stock market and any stock which makes its debut at a discount to the offer or placing price will trade under that cloud for some time to come.

From the point of view of the vendors of the stock, a huge premium represents to them a lost opportunity cost, in that the company has been sold too cheaply. For any investors it represents a bonanza of instant profits, which many will be quick to realize, producing undesirable volatility in the stock.

The sponsors to the issue therefore attempt in most cases to manage the issue so that a moderate first day premium is achieved. And given the experience of the broking houses in this regard, it would be unreasonable to assume that a significant number of new issues are mispriced, although it does happen.

If a decent but not excessive first day premium is achieved, it is then more than likely to be maintained in the following weeks, leading to positive press coverage and generally positive sentiment towards the stock.

To achieve a first day premium, the market as a whole has to perceive the stock to be good value by one of any number of measures (see chapter 3). It is the job of the sponsor to the issue to agree with the vendors a price likely to be acceptable to the market. Institutions and sponsors are by now well accustomed to the horse trading which accompanies most new issues, with the buy side trying to force the price down and the advisers to the vendors holding out for a better valuation.

Sometimes this bargaining is made public after institutions stage a buying strike and issue prices have been reduced. In some cases the two sides are too far apart and the issue is subsequently pulled, as happened with BAS Group flotation. But little can be deduced from the mere fact that prices have been reduced at the last minute. Both Albright & Wilson and Filtronic Comtek had their prices reduced due to institutional pressure, and saw large first day profits for those who invested as a result. General Cable reduced its price from an indicated 225 to 260 pence to the 190 pence level, but still went to an immediate discount.

In some larger issues there is now a process imported into the UK from the US called the 'Green Shoe' whereby the amount of stock actually issued is not fixed, but has a variable element to cope with market demand. Under the Green Shoe additional stock up to a limit specified in the prospectus can be issued to satisfy greater than anticipated demand. This raises additional funds for the company, and means that initial interest from those investors who did not obtain stock in the issue process can be satisfied without a stock shortage producing an undesirably high premium.

Stabilization is a similar process whereby the market making arm of the sponsor to the issue can buy in or issue extra stock to satisfy market demand in the few weeks following the issue, thereby supporting the price if there is an unexpected wave of selling, and preventing a stock shortage if the demand for the stock is high. Stabilization notices have to be issued to the market, and the process can only be maintained for several weeks. Even without the formal stabilization process, it is often suspected that for smaller issues the same outcome is achieved by the market makers of the sponsor to the stock running a long or short book for a period to influence the price.

Why do issues go to a premium?

When an offer process is completed much attention is given to the level of under- or over-subscription. Any issue which is under-subscribed is in danger of trading at a discount because buyers have not been found for all the stock in the issue, and this is unlikely to inspire buyers in the aftermarket. The stock not applied for will usually be taken up by the institutional underwriters of the issue, if any. These will therefore be overweight in the stock and will look to cut their holdings at some point in the future.

This does not mean they will sell at a loss immediately, but it does leave a stock overhang in the market. Any time the share price rises to a level which means the underwriters can get out at no loss – in practice the issue price or slightly below, given that underwriting commissions vary between a usual 1 per cent and as much as 4 per cent – they will look to sell. The consequence of this is that the stock will struggle to achieve any share price growth until the underwriters have reduced their holdings.

Much attention is similarly focused on the level of over-subscription. This is where many investors make a fundamental mistake. Many new issues, especially privatizations and larger issues advertised to the general public, can be several times over-subscribed due to a flood of small applications. These have been prompted by some of the privatization give-aways of the 1980s and early 1990s.

However, private investors are in general net sellers in the after-market. Those applicants who have been disappointed in the issue and have not received any stock at all or have been scaled down do not buy in the aftermarket in any great numbers. The level of first day premium for a stock is determined by the extent to which institutions are prepared to buy in the aftermarket. On this depends the level of institutional over-subscription for an issue, which is almost always not publicly disclosed.

Many new issues, especially privatizations, intentionally under-allot stock to the institutions, forcing them to buy stock in the aftermarket. Institutions account for around 70 per cent of UK stock market holdings with the balance held by private clients, but those institutions are frequently allotted only 50 per cent of a new issue.

In the case of early privatizations, such as those of British Tele-com and the Water and Electricity issues, these institutions felt under pressure to pick up the stock on the first day of trading, when there was in fact a stock shortage as even those private investors who wanted to sell could not do so as they had not received their allotment letters. In later issues it was realized that there was no immediate need to go into the market as a steady stream of stock from private client stags would soon materialize.

Nevertheless, institutional willingness to pick up stock in the aftermarket is a crucial determinant of the trading pattern of a stock, in its first few weeks. If they have been under-allotted stock, institutions will be consistent buyers, especially of stocks large enough to figure in portfolio weightings. Many funds are now index funds which attempt to track the performance of a particular index such as the FT-SE 100 or All-Share, or S&P 500 in the US. Index funds may in some cases feel forced to pick up stock to balance their weightings.

Index funds may . . . feel forced to pick up stock to balance their weightings.

In the case of smaller issues, some institutions will not have been allocated stock they desired because it has gone to better clients of the broker handling the issue. In other placings they may not have

been offered the stock at all. For a smaller company, just one or two
institutional buyers who were impressed by the management at the
pre-issue roadshow can create a substantial stock shortage. Even a
unit trust fund will usually look to buy stock in parcels of not less
than £250,000.

IS STAGGING WORTH IT?

Stagging is the practice of investing in a new issue in the expectation that it will go to an early premium, and taking that profit at
the first opportunity, in some cases in the first minutes of dealing.
An age-old tradition in the broking community, and a practice
indulged in by many fund managers also, it was introduced to the
general public in the privatization boom of the late 1980s. The
give-away pricing of these issues virtually guaranteed instant profits and members of the public who had never held shares before
queued up at broking firms and banks' instant dealing services to
unload their allocations.

But is stagging really worth it? The consensus of opinion in the
market is that indiscriminate stagging of new issues is no longer
worth it, and some are to be avoided altogether.

The huge premiums enjoyed by the early privatizations are
unlikely to be repeated, not least because the offer process has
been modified to better reflect demand in the pricing. Book-build-
ing exercises, 'Green Shoes' and stabilization are all intended to
manage the new issue process more efficiently. Institutions now
indicate the level of their interest for any given price, so few issues
come to the market at a large discount to their perceived value in
the market, leading fund managers to 'fill their boots'. And it is
the level of institutional interest in the aftermarket which generally
dictates early pricing moves. Private clients are almost always net
sellers, demonstrating that stagging is still alive and well.

Nevertheless, some issues, usually smaller ones, are definitely
worth stagging. Unfortunately it often only becomes evident that
they are worth it after most of the applications have gone in, by
which time it is too late for most investors.

Most professional stags are therefore stockbrokers and others very close to the market, as they are in a position to gauge their own clients' level of interest in the issue, make some guess as to the level of aftermarket demand and put applications in at the last minute. It is also the case that many professionals in the market are now effectively prevented by their compliance officers from dealing in the market. Only new issues are exempt from these onerous regulations.

The classic signs of an issue likely to be stagged is one which has seen a lot of press coverage to bring it to the attention of the general public (financial journalists are far from blameless in this respect), and is in some high growth sector likely to attract attention and generate some excitement as to prospects. This leads to optimistic pricing in the market, as it is difficult to value a stock which is expected to deliver fast growth, especially if it does not have any already quoted equivalents. More conventional stocks have an upper level on their pricing as they either trade above established criteria, such as net asset value for property stocks, or become so expensive compared with other stocks in their sector that professional investors switch out. As small stocks are almost often placed firm with institutions, or a placing is combined with intermediaries offer there is also a far from level playing field in terms of allocations, which means those who want to be involved, but cannot obtain stock in the issue, must buy in the aftermarket.

Is there any evidence?

Of some 130 new issues of reasonable size on the UK market in 1993 and 1994, 44 achieved a premium at the end of the first day of trading of 10 per cent or more. Some 18, or just under 10 per cent of the total, managed nearly 20 per cent or more with the clear leader being Virtuality. Its shares achieved a first day premium of 70 per cent. But the majority of new issues saw a premium in single figures in percentage terms, which meant that stagging was not worthwhile given the risks and costs involved.

Costs

The biggest problem for the stag is that costs are relatively high
compared with the profit anticipated. For the long-term investor
expecting some capital growth from the stock, the spread and dealing commission on exit can be lived with, but for the short-term
seller they can have a severe impact on the profitability of the transaction. It is relatively unusual for a new issue to go to an immediate
premium of more than 10 per cent. Investors in new issues do not
pay commission on the way in, but pay on the way out. This is anything up to 1.65 per cent with a £30
minimum for private clients, and 0.1
to 0.25 per cent for institutions.

> **The biggest problem for the stag is that costs are relatively high compared with the profit anticipated.**

More important is the spread –
for most issues worth stagging the
market makers' spread will be up
to 5 per cent of the price or even
higher, depending on the size and
liquidity of the issue. If there is a lot of genuine two way business
(i.e. buying and selling interest) the market makers' spread generally narrows, as they are interested primarily in turnover. Slack
markets or illiquid stocks make for larger spreads as the market
makers look to protect themselves. Therefore commission and
spread can make up several per cent of the price of the stock, especially where small dealing sizes are the norm. Given that these
have to be deducted from a premium of probably no more than 10
per cent, unless the issue has been seriously mispriced, stags are
looking to make profits of only a few per cent on the sum invested.
It only takes a small setback in the market to see this evaporate.

Opportunity costs

Any issue worth stagging will almost by definition be over-subscribed, leading to a scaling down of allocations. However, in an
offer for sale the cheque for the full amount of stock applied for
has to accompany the application form. These cheques are cashed
and a return cheque sent out for any stock applied for but not allo-

cated with the allotment letter. Investors can be out of the money for several weeks, and in the case of the larger privatizations the huge sums withdrawn from accounts began to pose liquidity problems for the building societies.

In the case of these privatizations investors were frequently allocated only a small proportion of the stock they applied for. Although they saw a large first day premium on the stock they did get, usually any profit on that was eaten into by stockbrokers' minimum commission levels. More important, they also lost several weeks' interest on the whole sum withdrawn from the bank or building society. Taking this into account, overall profits on the transaction were slim indeed, and private investors began to realize that the bonanza was not all it appeared.

Given that stagging an issue is not an individual pursuit – it depends on order and application imbalances – the time money is tied up in an issue is crucial. In 1994 there were over 200 new issues in the UK, but investors in each one saw their money tied up for several weeks. The money available to each individual for stagging an issue could therefore only be deployed in a handful of these issues – probably no more than 20 at best.

It is therefore often the case that the opportunity to invest in otherwise attractive issues is passed up because a more likely stagging opportunity is in the pipeline. This feature of the market is responsible for some issues seeing much heavier applications than others, and issuers are well aware of it. Bringing a small issue to the market at the same time as a privatization would not pose a problem as the two appeal to different types of investors, but it is counter-productive for two large offers for sale to clash. Even institutional cash flow is not unending.

Is it better to wait?

Institutions, the only buyers in size in the aftermarket, have become wiser after their experience of privatizations and are now less inclined to go into the market on the first day of dealings like a thundering herd. There remains the danger of missing it and seeing the price go up seemingly for ever at the price of their funds' performance, but they have realized that one of the reasons for the huge apparent premiums on the first day was an order imbalance.

Everyone expects a substantial number of private investors to stag an issue if they can get the stock, but the problem for them is that they only receive their allotment letters in the post. Few are able to actually deal on day one even if they wanted to. Experience has shown that private client sales in large offers for sale dribble into the market over the few weeks following an issue, leading to relatively high liquidity, and for the institutions the opportunity to pick up stock without large buying orders distorting the market. The changing nature of the larger market for new issues has ensured that they are not artificially starved of stock to the same extent.

But are the stags selling themselves short? Many of the issues which have shown significant first day premiums have in fact gone on to perform very well in the weeks, months and years following the issue, meaning that the stags have missed an opportunity for greater profits in the long term. A random sample of new issues in 1994 showed that a significant proportion of those issues which saw a first day premium large enough to realize a profit also went on to perform very well for the rest of the year. Others performed disastrously after unexpected profits warnings – Drew Scientific achieved a first day premium of 43 per cent but later sank to less than 20 per cent of its issue price. Stagging is not always the wrong course of action.

IS IT WORTH GEARING UP?

If a new issue is going to go to a decent premium and you are guaranteed some stock, go for as much as possible, if necessary by borrowing from the bank to finance it. But bear in mind the caveat which applies to all new issues: if it is that good there will be so many applications that you will get very little stock. The problem with gearing up is that (i) banks tend to charge relatively large sums for short-term facilities, and also charge fees for the facility even if it is not drawn down, and (ii) bank managers are understandably cautious about advancing funds for what they consider speculation.

The better route is to deal through a broking firm which will lend money to its clients for this purpose. As it understands the market and its risks the rate of interest charged will probably be lower, although a margin of around 30 per cent would be required, possibly in the form of other stock holdings – a significant advantage. However, under current legislation a consumer credit licence is required to advance sums under £15,000, so the amount of stock applied for would have to be in excess of £20,000 for this route to be feasible.

> **Fairly large sums can be payable to organize the facility, which can easily erode any premium achieved.**

The trouble with gearing up is that fairly large sums can be payable to organize the facility, which can easily erode any premium achieved. As these facilities are by their nature short term, the stagger is under some pressure to sell.

THE GREY MARKET

The 'Grey Market' was originally the invention of the gilts market. It refers to the practice of dealing in stocks on a 'when issued' basis, that is before those who have applied for stock actually receive it. Gilt issues start dealing on a specific day in the same way as equities, but it has long been the practice for the players in the market to deal in entitlements to the stock beforehand. This is to be extended to equity new issues, and was allowed in the BSkyB issue. Those who had put in for stock, and those who thought they would not get the allocation they desired, were able to buy and sell in the market even before the price had been fixed. Dealing on this basis can be void if the issue is subsequently pulled. The Grey Market is therefore a very good indicator as to what price the stock will open at once formal dealings commence. However, as it is not as liquid, prices can be volatile and subject to some distortion.

'Designed to appeal to young and fast growing businesses.'

13

THE ALTERNATIVE INVESTMENT MARKET (AIM)

- **The New Investment Market**
- **What companies will be attracted?**
- **Listing rules relaxed**
- **Nominated advisers and brokers; trading**
- **Tax breaks**

THE NEW MARKET

The Alternative Investment Market (AIM) started trading in the UK in June 1995 with 10 companies listed initially, although a much more substantial number are expected by the year end. Around 100 stocks can be expected to trade on the market in the short term, compared with well over 2,000 with a full listing.

To some extent the AIM market reflects the success of the NASDAQ market in the United States, and there has been talk of setting up an EASDAQ market in Europe.

The AIM market reflects the success of the NASDAQ market in the United States.

The market was set up in response to demands for a lightly regulated market for smaller companies which did not have the onerous listing requirements of a full listing. It is difficult to bring a company to the market for less than £300,000, according to some brokers. Costs to bring a company to the AIM market can be expected to be under £100,000 if no new equity is raised. At least one broker is offering a package for less than £50,000.

AIM will replace the Unlisted Securities Market (USM), soon to become defunct, and will substantially replace the Rule 4.2 market in that most of the liquid stocks currently traded under Rule 4.2 will probably wish to graduate to AIM.

The Rule 4.2 market is another lightly regulated market where most shares are effectively traded on a matched bargain basis by stockbrokers. Of several hundred companies with permission to trade from the Stock Exchange, some 70 account for the bulk of trading and have an active market made in their shares to some extent. Other shares under 4.2 trade only a handful of times a year.

Rule 4.2 stocks enjoyed a flurry of interest as the USM was closed for new entrants, and while the arrangements for AIM were

---

MEMORY CORPORATION

The attractions of these smaller companies should not be underestimated. One of the very best performing new issues of the last few years has been Memory Corporation, a small computer hardware manufacturer which has developed a method of repairing defective memory chips.

Memory Corporation was worthy of note not just because of its attractive product, but also because despite a Rule 4.2 quote it had relatively high liquidity with the shares frequently traded in blocks of 50,000 or more.

Memory Corporation shares were floated at 45 pence, opened at 90, and hit 240 within a few months. However, they slumped to 150 pence on news that the product was not as effective in tests as some had hoped.

The stock demonstrated both the attractions of smaller companies – the chance to get in on the ground floor of a potentially high performing company – and also some of the downside. The company's product was at an early stage of development so sentiment was important and any setback potentially disastrous. What Memory Corp shares did have, however, was liquidity.

For many AIM companies, getting out if it turns sour could be very difficult. A stock with a large free float and two market makers could be a much better investment proposition than one traded only on a matched bargain basis.

finalized. In that period some very attractive companies came to the market, and despite the apparent risks of smaller companies, these Rule 4.2 stocks had fewer flops than the wider market.

WHAT COMPANIES WILL BE ATTRACTED?

According to the Stock Exchange, the new AIM market is designed to appeal to young and fast growing businesses, including start-ups, management buyouts and buyins, family owned businesses and former Business Expansion Scheme companies.

It also stresses that AIM is designed for professional or experienced investors who understand the nature of the market and are prepared to accept the potential risks and rewards.

In practice the AIM market looks set to attract fairly entrepreneurial management teams who, for reasons of size, cost, or inability to comply with listing rules, are unable to obtain a full listing. For most companies a full listing would be a more attractive proposition because some institutions have expressed concern about the more lax listing rules for AIM companies and could be unwilling to invest. On the other hand, trading on AIM could result in a slightly higher profile.

LISTING RULES RELAXED

Companies seeking access to AIM are not required to have reached a certain size, have a defined number of shares in public hands or prove a lengthy trading history. However, their shares must be freely transferable and they must retain a nominated adviser or and nominated broker.

The Stock Exchange does not apply any stricter rules to companies without a trading record, but directors of those with a revenue earning history of less than two

There are no rules governing the methods of issuing or distributing AIM securities to the market.

years must agree not to dispose of their interest for one year after joining the market.

Crucially, there are no rules governing the methods of issuing or distributing AIM securities to the market.

ROLE OF THE NOMINATED ADVISER

The role of the company's professional advisers is also changed in relationship to AIM.

All companies are required to have a nominated adviser at all times. However, the crucial difference between a nominated adviser and a sponsor to a fully listed company is that the adviser is not required to confirm that any relevant requirements have been met, and do not perform a due diligence function on behalf of the Stock Exchange. For instance, nominated advisers do not have to back up profits forecasts.

However, advisers with a reputation to maintain will have an incentive to undertake some form of due diligence investigation even if not specifically required by the Stock Exchange. Certain Stock Exchange criteria have to be satisfied before a broking firm can obtain nominated adviser status.

All companies traded on AIM are also required to have a nominated broker to support trading in the company's shares. The firm is required to use its 'best endeavours' to maintain a market in the company's shares and find matched bargain business. This does not apply if there is a market maker in the stock, and in practice it looks as if most AIM stocks will have a full time market maker.

If a company loses its adviser or broker it runs the risk of losing its AIM quote if a replacement is not appointed within a month.

TAX BREAKS

Companies traded on AIM will be able to offer tax breaks not available to investors in fully listed shares.

Majority owners will gain relief from inheritance tax, which could result in some of the family owned companies which still exist on the stock market inhabiting AIM in future. This could be advantageous for investors in fully listed companies, but beware of AIM. Companies still run as a family business have different investment objectives than those which are fully independent.

Investors will be able to take advantage of rollover relief. It will be possible to defer capital gains by reinvesting the proceeds of the sale of shares in one AIM company in another one, with no capital gains paid until the final sale. Also, losses can be offset against income tax.

But bear in mind that however advantageous the tax breaks on an investment are, tax relief only maximizes gains and takes some of the pain out of losses. It does nothing to influence either in the first place.

CHECKLIST

In addition to all of the usual criteria to apply to any new issue, bear in mind the following with AIM stocks.

i   *Who is the broker? Does the firm have a reputation for smaller company issues, and can it attract any institutional business?*

ii   *What is the level of free float (the proportion of shares not held by management, family and institutions)?*

iii   *Will there be a market maker in the stock independent of the nominated broker?*

iv   *What is the likely liquidity of the shares?*

v   *Check the prospectus carefully. The inherent risks of these smaller stocks can be higher.*

APPENDIX

WHAT TO LOOK FOR IN THE PROSPECTUS

Most new issue prospectuses now follow roughly the same format in order to enhance the attractions to the international investor base. Legal and other rules ensure that the prospectus contains a mass of information of little actual relevance to most investors; many of the statements can be taken as read because an issue will not get off the ground without them (but note extra care should be taken with AIM documentation).

Most information in a new issue prospectus is never read, even by the most diligent of investors. Summarized below is what to look for, and where. The format is generally as follows for a UK offer:

Basic offer statistics

- Market capitalization following the issue
- Offer price or range
- Number of shares being offered
- Number of shares in issue following the float
- Net proceeds
- Earnings forecast
- Dividend yield
- Dividend cover

Notes: From the number of shares being offered and the number in issue following the float the extent to which existing shareholders control the company can be deduced. Is the net proceeds of the offer too small? (Most of the shares are being sold by existing shareholders rather than for the value of the company.) Is there a profits (earnings) forecast? (The absence of one raises questions.) The p/e ratio and dividend yield at the issue price should not be out of line with the market.

Timetable

- Last date for receipt of retail offer applications
- Last date for institutional applications or indications of interest
- Announcement of price and basis of allocations
- Dealings commence

Notes: Are retail investors required to submit applications well before institutional investors? Is there a long time before the closure of the offer, announcement of price (if not fixed) and dealings. Will retail investors know the level of allocations before dealings commence?

Summary of business

- Overview of business, its strengths and brief profits history
- Profits forecast, current trading statement
- Basis of offer – domestic/retail/international split
- Use of proceeds
- Dividend policy
- Large shareholders following the offer

Notes: Is there a risk warning? Are retail investors favoured or discriminated against? Are large shareholders selling out, and who will control the company after the flotation?

Further details

- More detailed analysis of the business including its history, subsidiaries and properties owned if appropriate
- Directors and their biographies
- Profits history

Notes: Check the directors' biographies. How long have they been with the company? What prior experience do they have? Are they already known to the market (a big plus point for the stock)?

Pro forma financial information

Much the same as a normal set of full accounts for the company. Pro forma means what the group will look like after the flotation.

Notes: Look at the accounting policies, particularly depreciation, accounting for brand names (a contentious issue), writing off or otherwise of research and development expenditure, capitalization of interest, ACT write-offs. The balance sheet should give a net asset value and cash position.

Additional information

In many ways the additional information section of a prospectus makes the most interesting reading, as it contains all the information the lawyers require to be in the prospectus, but the company would prefer not to highlight.

- Directors' share options
- Directors' interests
- Any other options over the shares
- Large shareholdings
- Directors' service contracts
- Material contracts between directors and the company
- Underwriting agreements – including details of commission paid to intermediaries to sell the offer
- Litigation
- Total costs of the issue – i.e. what goes to the advisers
- Net proceeds
- Whether any directors have skeletons in the cupboard
- Post balance sheet events

WHAT TO LOOK FOR IN THE PROSPECTUS –
US VERSION

Virtually all US IPO prospectuses follow the same format regardless of the stock exchange the shares are to be traded on. In common with prospectuses in other countries the document contains a mass of regulatory detail of little interest to most investors, who rarely struggle beyond the first page, instead relying on the recommendation of their broker.

Front cover

- What is the price range?
- How much stock is on offer?
- Is there a 'Green Shoe'/Stabilization provision (there usually is)?
- What stock exchange will the shares be traded on?
- Is there a risk warning?
- Who is selling?
- Will the company receive any of the proceeds?

Notes: Look for the market capitalization – is it too small for the stock to have a liquid aftermarket? Is the price range comparable with other stocks in the sector? but remember the price and the amount of stock on offer can be changed at the last minute depending on demand.

PAGE 1 – Summary of the company. Few investors read beyond the first page!

Summary

- Dependence on certain products/customers
- Key personnel
- Future sales by shareholders
- Control by one or more shareholders
- Check for section entitled Use of Proceeds
- Dividend policy

Note: Look out for the control by one or more shareholders. It is common for an IPO to result in effective control by the previous owner, but this is not a critical factor. The IPO is often used to set a market price for the stock, in anticipation of a larger secondary offer in due course. An extensive set of risk warnings should not necessarily be construed as a warning not to buy the stock. All of this may be in the price, and anyway they are there to satisfy regulators rather than advise investors.

The rest of the prospectus

Note: This section contains hugely detailed financial information on the company, which few will read. But look out for details of:

- Directors' employment agreements
- Share option plans
- Patents
- Licensing agreements
- Litigation

GLOSSARY

ADR: American Depositary Receipt. Mechanism for allowing shares in a company domiciled in one country to be traded in the US without producing settlement problems. A US custodian holds the shares in the company and issues ADRs with rights to the shares which can then be freely traded in the US without having to settle transactions in the company's home market.

AIM: The Alternative Investment Market. New market for smaller and growing companies set up in the UK in 1995 to replace the USM (Unlisted Securities Market).

Allotment Letter: In UK only, a document signalling the number of shares allotted to an applicant in a new issue. Tradeable in this form for several months until the company's share register has been compiled.

Covenant: Term for the quality of a tenant in a rental property.

Dow Jones Industrial Average: An index of the top 30 stocks traded on the New York Stock Exchange. One of the most quoted but not particularly representative indices.

FT-SE 100: The *Financial Times*–Stock Exchange index of the top 100 quoted companies in the UK by market capitalization. The FT-SE accounts for around half the total market capitalization and half the market trading volume in the UK.

GDR: Global Depositary Receipt. Similar to ADR but tradeable globally.

Grey Market: Term in UK for trading in securities before they have officially been issued.

Intermediaries Offer: Sale of shares to larger private investors by either reserving a proportion of the shares specifically for the intermediaries offer or allowing private investors to participate in the institutional offer.

Investment Trust: UK name for investment fund constituted as a company in its own right, holding equity portfolio and paying out majority of income as dividends.

IPO: Initial Public Offering. US term for new issue, now generic term in global market for the first time a company sells equity shares for listing on a recognized stock exchange.

Market Maker: Securities firm in the UK (and on NASDAQ) who runs a book in one or more shares. Required to continually maintain a screen-based buying and selling price for the shares, to provide a liquid market.

Market Capitalization: The total value of shares in issue of a company multiplied by the share price. Note that the market capitalisation is not the same as the 'free float' which may be lower if only a proportion of the shares has been floated.

MBO/MBI: Management Buy out/Buy in. The purchase of a company either by its existing management team (MBO) or a team replacing the existing management (MBI). MBOs and MBIs often seek a market listing within a few years to provide an exit for venture capital investors and to repay debt.

NASDAQ: National Association of Securities Dealers Automated Quote. Rival to NYSE, comprising a large number of technology issues.

NAV: Net Asset Value, usually calculated per share. The assets of the company less liabilities as stated in the balance sheet. A measure of value, usually in connection with property companies and investment trusts.

NYSE: New York Stock Exchange.

Offer for Sale: Sale of shares by offering them to institutions and the general public via advertisements in newspapers, television, and direct marketing.

Pathfinder: Early version of prospectus, omitting some details on issue pricing which are decided on at the last minute.

P/E Ratio: Price/earnings ratio. The ratio of the share price to the earnings (profits after tax) per share. Earnings per share is the total after tax profits divided by the number of shares in issue. The p/e ratio is one of the standard measures of share price value.

Placing: Sale of shares by offering them to selected investors, with interest solicited by brokers to the issue.

Prospectus: Marketing document for a new issue, containing financial and other details on the company, and details on the number of shares to be issued and price.

Red Herring: US name for pathfinder prospectus.

S&P 500: Standard & Poors index of the top 500 stocks on the New York Stock Exchange. More representative of the wider market than the Dow Jones.

SEC: The Securities and Exchange Commission, US market regulator.

SFA: The Securities and Futures Authority, UK market regulator.

Specialist: US equivalent on NYSE of market maker in the UK. Does not maintain a continuous quote but matches buy and sell orders.

Stagging, Stag: The practice of applying for shares in a new issue with the intention of selling as soon as possible in the aftermarket to realize a profit.

Stock Exchange: In the context, the International Stock Exchange of the United Kingdom and Ireland. Also runs the AIM market and USM. Until recently the sole market for shares in the UK.

Trade Sale: Selling a company privately to another company in the same business, rather than floating its shares.

Venture Capital: Funds providing either start-up (rarer) or development capital for companies,often by taking an equity stake before the company is quoted on any stock exchange. Venture capital funds are usually looking for an exit from their investment within five years.

Warrant: Derivative security giving the holder the right but not the obligation to subscribe for shares in a company at some point in the future, usually three to seven years from issue. Warrants can be traded.

Yield: The dividend payment per share expressed as a percentage of the share price. Usually calculated gross to take account of any tax deductions.

INDEX

Also available from Pitman Publishing

THE INVESTOR'S GUIDE TO OFFSHORE INVESTMENT

International Tactics for the Active Investor

Offshore investment brings a wealth of opportunity to the investor who is serious about taking full advantage of every investment, and who wants to retain as much of their earnings as possible. Successful offshore investment will allow the guerilla investor to access more markets, spread their risk, pay less tax, retain anonymity and stay one step ahead of all those with an interest in their earnings.

The Investor's Guide to Offshore Investment takes the lid of this little-understood market and provides you with the vital inside knowledge and secret tactics you need to break into (perfectly legal) offshore investment, ranging from how to make your investments work harder for you, to the various uses for tax havens, (i.e., protecting your assets from lawsuits, governments, creditors and spouses).

Make your own plans, diversify abroad and become the master of your own destiny; become an offshore investor.

£50.00 Hardback ISBN 0273 61593 9

Dear Pitman Publishing Customer

We are delighted to announce a special free service for all of our customers.

Simply complete this form and return it to the FREEPOST address overleaf to receive:

- Free Customer Newsletter
- Free Information Service
- Exclusive Customer Offers – which have included free software, videos and relevant products
- Opportunity to take part in product development sessions
- The chance for you to write about your own business experience and become one of our respected authors

Fill this in now and return it to us (no stamp needed in the UK) to join our customer information service.

Name: _____ Position: _____

Company/Organisation: _____

Address (including postcode): _____

Country: _____

Telephone: _____ Fax: _____

Nature of business: _____

Title of book purchased: _____

ISBN (printed on back cover): [0] [2] [7] [3] [ ] [ ] [ ] [ ]

Comments: _____

-------------------- | Fold Here Then Staple Once | --------------------

We would be very grateful if you could answer these questions to help us with market research.

1 Where/How did you hear of this book?

[ ] in a bookshop

[ ] in a magazine/newspaper
   (please state which):

_____

[ ] information through the post

[ ] recommendation from a colleague

[ ] other (please state which):

_____

2 Where did you buy this book?

[ ] Direct from Pitman Publishing

[ ] From a bookclub

[ ] From a bookshop (state which)

_____

3 Which newspaper(s)/magazine(s) do you read regularly?

_____

4 When buying a business book which factors influence you most?
(Please rank in order)

[ ] recommendation from a colleague

[ ] price

[ ] content

[ ] recommendation in a bookshop

[ ] author

[ ] publisher

[ ] title

[ ] other(s):

_____

5 Is this book a

[ ] personal purchase?

[ ] company purchase ?

6 Would you be prepared to spend a few minutes talking to our customer services staff to help with product development?

[ ] yes

[ ] no

The Business Publisher

Written for managers competing in today's tough business world, our books will give you a competitive edge by showing you how to:

- increase quality, efficiency and productivity throughout your organisation
- use both proven and innovative management techniques
- improve your management skills and those of your staff
- implement winning customer strategies

In short they provide concise, practical information that you can use every day to manage more effectively

----

WC2E 9BR, UK

LONDON

128 Long Acre

FREEPOST

Pitman Professional Publishing

Free Information Service

No stamp
necessary
in the UK